Technology as a Catalyst for School Communities

Beyond Boxes and Bandwidth

Mary Burns and K. Victoria Dimock

ROWMAN & LITTLEFIELD EDUCATION
Lanham • New York • Toronto • Plymouth, UK

Published in the United States of America
by Rowman & Littlefield Education
A Division of Rowman & Littlefield Publishers, Inc.
A wholly owned subsidiary of The Rowman & Littlefield Publishing Group, Inc.
4501 Forbes Boulevard, Suite 200, Lanham, Maryland 20706
www.rowmaneducation.com

Estover Road
Plymouth PL6 7PY
United Kingdom

British Library Cataloguing in Publication Information Available

Library of Congress Cataloging-in-Publication Data

Burns, Mary, 1962-
  Technology as a catalyst for school communities : beyond boxes and bandwidth
/ Mary Burns and K. Victoria Dimock.
      p. cm.
  Includes bibliographical references and index.
  ISBN-13: 978-1-57886-665-6 (cloth : alk. paper)
  ISBN-10: 1-57886-665-0 (cloth : alk. paper)
  ISBN-13: 978-1-57886-666-3 (pbk. : alk. paper)
  ISBN-10: 1-57886-666-9 (pbk. : alk. paper)
  1. Educational technology—Case studies. 2. Educational
  change—Case studies. I. Dimock, K. Victoria. II. Title.
  LB1028.3.B87 2007
  371.33—dc22   2007038197

⊗™ The paper used in this publication meets the minimum requirements of
American National Standard for Information Sciences—Permanence of Paper
for Printed Library Materials, ANSI/NISO Z39.48-1992.
Manufactured in the United States of America.

Dedication

As we began writing this book, Mary's mother was diagnosed with Alzheimer's disease. Vicki, unfortunately, preceded her in terms of experience with this disease. Her mother had suffered for years from Alzheimer's. The paradox became increasingly obvious. We were writing what was essentially a book about learning while our mothers struggled without success to retain knowledge that took seventy to eighty years to accumulate but only a few years to be destroyed by this mysterious disease.

As Mary shifted between her roles as daughter-caretaker and writer, we became aware of learning's inextricable link to human existence. As our mothers lost the ability to recall, reminisce, create, analyze, memorize, and communicate, they progressively seemed to lose part of their humanity and their joy for living. And as we took care of our mothers and as we wrote, we came to realize that one of the greatest gifts of living is the ability to continuously learn. We humans are learners. It is the ability to learn, think, feel, and reflect that marks the difference between living and merely existing.

Alzheimer's robs its victims of accumulated memories, of accomplishments, and of competence—in short, many of the things that make us human. Although we have ceased to exist in the minds of our mothers, their life lessons and their love will remain with us always. We dedicate this book to our mothers, Josephine Dimock and Margaret Burns, and to the millions like them who struggle with Alzheimer's.

Contents

Foreword

Have you ever had the experience of thinking that you know a lot, perhaps know all there is to know, about a topic or subject, and then pow! You bump into a new angle, perspective, or analysis that provides a brilliant new understanding of the topic.

I just had that experience.

I believe profoundly in the idea of communities of practice/professional learning communities (PLC) and the potential that this way of working has to increase teacher and administrator effectiveness. As the label suggests, a professional learning community's purpose, or mission, is the continuous learning of the professionals in the school. The research on PLC reveals five components that comprise a PLC. These are

- Shared beliefs, values, and vision
- Shared and supportive leadership
- Collective learning and its application
- Supportive conditions (both structural and relational)
- Peers supporting peers in improving their practice (Hord, 2004)

I thought I had these components well understood, especially the component of collective learning and its application, until I reviewed Mary Burns' and Victoria Dimock's manuscript. Their analysis of the three stages of community development peeled another layer off the collective learning component and the overall concept of PLC/communities of practice. I gained a richer, deeper, new meaning both conceptually and operationally of school learning communities.

This foreword is not the place to explain how communities of interest lead to communities of learning, and then to communities of practice.

Burns and Dimock do so in this book. From their careful observations of three schools engaged in technology-oriented professional development, and the authors' thoughtful exploration of the schools' subsequent work in implementing technology-enhanced instructional strategies, we gain important insights about these three stages of community and how their educator members learn about technology in classroom instruction, and about how to use it to increase students' learning.

In these three school cases, we live the experiences of the educators as they are alternately frustrated and delighted, uncomfortable and pleased, reluctant and enthusiastic while learning in a social setting with their colleagues and peers. Learning in community, solving the problems of applying their learning in their classrooms, sharing early disappointments and eventual successes—all are revealed to us in this book. The reader gains powerful new understandings and insights from the stories of these learning communities of educators.

Of particular concern to school improvers is the initial stage, the community of interest. It is at this crucial point that the educator is persuaded or propelled into embracing professional development's learning activities, or rejects them. Thus, this stage is critical to the success of the subsequent stages. It makes excellent sense to provide a community context in which those learning about technology might meet their learning challenges with support from other learners, and thrive.

But, as we learn from this book, community-based learning has many advantages across the lifespan of the school, and we are introduced to them by Mary Burns and Victoria Dimock. This book warrants a place in the library of all who seek to better understand how to use community learning to increase educators' effectiveness and, subsequently, students' successful learning.

Shirley M. Hord
Scholar Emerita
Southwest Educational Development Laboratory
Austin, Texas
May 2007

Acknowledgments

We gratefully acknowledge the contributions of our colleagues at the Southwest Educational Development Laboratory who worked with us on the Applying Technology to Restructuring Learning project (ATRL): Sharon Adams, Jackie Burniske, Jackie Cuevas, Marilyn Heath, Danny Martinez, and the late Jim Zuhn. As we worked together to design and deliver the ATRL professional development and to support the work of the teachers and administrators in the schools in which we worked, we, too, became a community of practice. We studied together, planned together, fought through conflicts, and supported one another in our difficult work as external facilitators of school change.

We also acknowledge, with deep respect and gratitude, the hard work and willingness of all the teachers, administrators, technology coordinators, parents, and colleagues at the schools in which we worked to open them to change. Without them and their unceasing dedication to improve education for the children they serve, this book would not have been possible.

1

Applying Technology to Restructuring Learning

Coming together is a beginning. Staying together is progress. Working together is success.

—Henry Ford

This is a book about change—personal change, classroom change, and institutional change—affecting teachers, students, administrators, and the professional-development providers who worked with them. It tells the story of how a group of educators resisted change, adapted to change, embraced it, and eventually were united by it.

BACKGROUND

The stories told in this book come from teachers and principals working in low-income communities to integrate computer technology into their classrooms to promote more effective, learner-centered instruction. Computers were becoming increasingly commonplace in many low-income schools, and states and districts increasingly mandated their use. Because of these administrative mandates, together with computers' novelty, seeming complexity, and growing prevalence, computer technology represented a crucible of sorts for many teachers. Computers inspired reactions ranging from fear, loathing, fascination, interest, and uncertainty to enthusiasm—often in combination.

As with many educational innovations, district leaders viewed computers as tools to promote instructional reform. In fact, many leaders considered computers the essential tool to promote such reform. By installing equipment and training teachers to use technology, it was hypothesized that teachers would not only use computers, but use them to teach differently so that students could learn in new and improved ways.

The goal of using computers to reform teachers' instructional practices promised to be hard to achieve. The schools in question were poor, "at-risk," and/or "low-performing," based on attendance rates, student demographics, and state test scores. Most of the classrooms had a high student–computer ratio: 25:1 on average, and in some instances 35:1. Teacher demographics spanned the experience continuum, creating a difficult professional-development task: many teachers had more than twenty years' experience, whereas many others were first-year teachers. Would the "veterans" be resistant to change? Would the novices be too inexperienced to implement the types of instructional changes promoted by the professional development?

PROGRESS DESPITE CHALLENGES

The infrastructure of the professional development was carefully fashioned. Administrator support was secured, and at least twenty-five teacher participants ensured a critical mass and created a core of innovative practitioners who would create systemic change on a campus level.

Despite this careful planning, the problems at some of these schools exceeded the scope of technology and pedagogy. Many students were "at risk," but so too, it seemed, were many teachers—they found no joy in either teaching or learning and seemed to have no sense of shared purpose with colleagues or students.[1]

Yet, over the course of two years, important changes took place. Teachers were becoming facilitators and mentors. Students were active and engaged and were using computers for research, problem solving, and creative expression. The distance between teachers and students—academic, emotional, and physical—had been bridged, and teachers, with regard to technology, became co-learners with students. Autonomy, decentralization, and responsibility appeared to be the new defining instructional characteristics. Teachers reported that students' work was better and discipline problems had diminished, and many confided that they enjoyed teaching again for the first time in many years.

COMING TOGETHER

Teacher technology use, change in instructional practice, and new classroom dynamics represented dramatic and positive outcomes that had been desired for the project. But something more extraordinary and unanticipated occurred during the two years of professional development. At each campus, teachers began to meet on a regular basis, outside the regular professional-development sessions, to support one another in improving their teaching. Teachers were forming their own communities.

At some campuses, this community formation arose from a purposeful and collective desire to improve student performance. In others, communities resulted from a need for a safe harbor amid great change. Some communities were highly structured, robust, and vibrant; others were still in the formative stage. Some included all teachers in the project; others were composed of smaller subgroups. Sometimes, the same teachers populated both kinds of groups. Although the configuration, composition, and purpose of these communities varied across and within schools, on every campus, teachers began to learn together, talk together, plan together, and teach together. They were no longer working alone; they were working together.

Communities of Interest

The formation of these communities evolved in a gradual, incremental, and distinct fashion that can be described as having three stages (see figure 1.1). Teachers first came together in *communities of interest*. This stage provided the social context within which learners could connect to one another via a shared professional interest—computer technology and the technology skills and content offered within professional-development sessions, particularly in relation to certain content areas. In these sessions, interaction and connection were founded on shared professional and intellectual pursuits. Such interaction and shared interest had limited spillover beyond the actual sessions. Nonetheless, this type of community formation, brief and preliminary, was foundational in that it served as the first stage in the community-of-practice formation.

Communities of Learning

As teachers became more involved in the professional development, these communities of interest moved beyond the confines of professional-development sessions to the actual school day, evolving into

Community of Interest

Community of Learning

Community of Practice

Figure 1.1.

communities of learning, the defining characteristic of which was communication. Teachers began to talk about instruction, curriculum, and technology. They came together to reflect on their practice and were increasingly deliberative and deliberate in terms of pedagogical decisions. Teachers were having more discussions with colleagues about instructional practice and more often shared student work with colleagues.

Communities of Practice

In the final stage, reflection and discussion, although still present, were transformed into action. Teachers formed *communities of practice* in which cooperation and collaboration were the prime characteristics. Teachers were not just talking about instructional ideas; they were working with colleagues on curriculum development, lesson plans, and activities. They were co-teaching students, soliciting student input in order to improve the learning process, helping other teachers manage the logistical and conceptual challenges associated with technology, and changing instruction—and they supported one another as they did so. They were not just learning from and with one another and their students; they were working jointly with fellow teachers and students.

Communities Defined

Despite the prevalence of the terms *communities of learning* and *communities of practice*, educators often lack clear understanding of why such communities are important, what constitute the defining and distinguishing features of each, and why understanding those distinctions holds practical implications for schools. Although the terms *communities of learning* and *communities of practice* are often used interchangeably or synonymously (Hord, 1997; Wenger, 1998), and although the groups they define do share common characteristics and goals, the experience of the authors suggests that the two terms reflect real differences that go beyond simple semantic parsing and that actually impact the type of change that occurs within an organizational setting.

Community (of any type) is desirable because it provides emotional, logistical, and procedural supports for its members in the pursuit of common interests and goals, transforming an undertaking from the individual to the shared realm. Communities of learning and communities of practice, as mentioned earlier, begin as communities of *interest*—purposeful collections and networks of professionals formed around a "joint enterprise" (Wenger, 1998), an idea, innovation, common problem, or interest that functions as the collective brain or soul of an organization. Both types of community discussed here are characterized by knowledge generation and shared learning. Both are goal-oriented, and the attainment of goals is facilitated by the trust, mutual support, and open communication that form the basis of a community. Both make public the private, embedded, and tacit professional knowledge of individuals within the group (Fullan, 2001).

In a community of learning, however, the focus is on cognition and affect, on learning (on the acquisition, synthesis, accommodation, assimilation, generation, and transmission of new information and knowledge), and on the participant as a learner. Learning, in short, is the goal. Although new learning may be translated into actual classroom practice—and that result is often assumed—teachers may participate in communities of learning without discernible or deliberate impacts of new learning on their practice.

In contrast, *communities of practice* are characterized by greater *cooperation* and *collaboration* among community members. These terms' original meanings, "operating together" and "working together," suggest a practice-based focus on shared action. It is this practice-based focus—this "working together," the authors believe—that essentially distinguishes communities of practice from communities of learning. Communities of practice are task- and performance-oriented, concentrating on application of knowledge and focused on teacher behavior. Such groups engage the teacher as a doer, an actor, and a practitioner. Although teacher affect and cognition are certainly necessary ingredients in a community of practice, the emphasis is on action, on behavior, on transforming new learning into informed practice, and on instructional change.

Within communities of learning, a new professional vision or set of values is often identified, shared, and communicated. The implementation of this new learning, the focus on application, and the supports created to sustain the new practice mark the transition to a community of practice. Communities of learning and communities of practice can coexist, overlap, and be populated by the same subset of individuals. However, even though a community of learning is an absolute requisite for a community of practice, it does not, in and of itself, constitute a community of practice.

Communities of practice can yield several tangible benefits that promote change on a classroom or school-wide level. Such groups help to reinforce many of the skills, concepts, and new understandings that teachers learn in professional-development sessions. They provide a social context that allows for the translation of learning into practice. By working with colleagues, teachers can personalize and adapt new skills and concepts to their classrooms, gain new ideas and perspectives from colleagues, and think critically about curricula, methodology, assessment practices, and their relationships with students. Communities of practice help to build a public repertoire of agreed-upon good practice. Most saliently, professional isolation can be replaced by cooperation and collaboration, laying the groundwork for a collective ethos of professional sharing, feedback, and alignment between vision and actual classroom practice, all of which can result in greater change at a school level. Through this formation of community, schools can become better professional places for teachers and better places for students (Brandt, 1992).

WORKING TOGETHER

What created these changes? What accounted for this transformation from, in many instances, isolated, sterile, or not fully actualized learning environments to more dynamic classrooms in which students were active, engaged, and excited about learning, and in which collaboration prevailed? What contributed to this dramatic shift in technology use, instruction, and educational ethos? And how and why did teachers come together, work together, and sustain their school-based communities?

The answers to these questions lie in the type of professional development in which teachers were engaged and the ways in which technology was used within that professional development, coupled with the characteristics of the individual campuses. These topics will be examined throughout this book.

READING GUIDE

The following chapters discuss the characteristics of the professional development and the unique campus-based conditions that propelled teachers to move from an individual practice to one that was more collective, and from an ethic that was based more on private needs and activity to one based on public needs (Riel & Polin, 2004) and common work: in short, toward the formation of campus-based communities of practice. Whereas for the authors the innovation around which professional development occurred was computer technology, for readers it may be an inquiry-based science program, a new reading program, or a hands-on math program. Many of the experiences and "lessons learned" discussed in this book will hold true, no matter the innovation.

Chapter 2 describes the professional development in which teachers were engaged, outlining best practices in professional development, regardless of the focus of that professional development. Chapter 3 discusses how the professional development's focus on computers made changing technology use common among teachers and served as a catalyst for community formation among them, as well as between teachers and students. Chapters 4, 5, and 6 provide site-specific case studies of three of the six campuses, looking at the events and factors at each that contributed to instructional change and community formation. Chapter 7 offers some guiding principles for administrators and professional-development specialists wishing to promote instructional change and community formation in their own schools or districts.

The stories told in this book also show that there is no one template for change or for the creation of communities of practice that spawn and incubate such change. Numerous factors can contribute to successful adoption of new practices. The unique character of individuals, groups, and systems ensures that no two models or contributing causes of communities of practice are identical. The schools profiled in this book differed in the degree and kinds of communities they created, as well as in the role that technology played in their transformation. Through the stories of change on three school campuses, it is hoped that the "how" and "why" of such changes will become clear and that administrators and professional-development providers can replicate some of the strategies outlined here in their own schools with similar results.

NOTE

1. Roland S. Barth uses the term *at risk* to refer to teachers who exhibit similar characteristics of isolation and little opportunity or interest in continued learning.

2

Teacher-centered Professional Development

Real learning gets to the heart of what it means to be human. Through learning we re-create ourselves. Through learning we become able to do something we were never able to do. Through learning we extend our capacity to create. . . . There is within each of us a deep hunger for this type of learning.

—Peter Senge, *The Fifth Discipline*

What do teachers need to emerge from largely isolated private practice toward a more public one based on professional cooperation, collaboration, and community? How can school administrators and teacher educators create such communities of practice within their campuses?

One answer is to foster an environment that encourages and rewards professional learning and collaborative practice. As part of this milieu, teachers must be provided with collaborative learning opportunities that help them to address a particular classroom need and to achieve a particular set of professional goals. In essence, teachers must be provided with professional development that is teacher-centered.

TEACHER-CENTERED PROFESSIONAL DEVELOPMENT DEFINED

Over the past twenty years or so, educators have become increasingly aware of the cognitive and emotional needs of students as learners. This new awareness has spawned a push toward student-centered and differentiated instruction, resulting in numerous accommodations to promote student learning both collectively and individually. Yet many school districts have been less aware of teachers as learners, with needs similar to those of students. Consequently, in-service teacher education remains remarkably non–teacher-centered and non-differentiated, with few accommodations for teachers' needs as learners.

Professional-development choices are often still made without the voice of the teacher and without the professional-development provider having firsthand knowledge of the realities of teachers' classrooms. And teacher professional development frequently embodies practices that are ill suited to optimal learning. Although, for example, an inspiring speaker may do a wonderful job of generating initial enthusiasm, or the demonstration of a science kit may give teachers new ideas, such professional development often involves teachers assuming a passive role, interacting minimally with peers, and having little or no opportunity during the professional-development session to practice what they have heard or seen. In the case of technology, school- and district-based professional-development programs often consist of single workshops focused on skills development or knowledge acquisition, with little understanding of the issues surrounding technology integration in the classroom.

When teachers are not seen as learners, their individual and developmental needs are not taken into account. District-based professional-development activities may be identical for all teachers in all schools. Scaffolding or follow-up support for teacher learning may not exist. It is expected that, from the workshop, the teacher has learned all he or she needs in order to master the innovation in the classroom. The message, perhaps inadvertent but nonetheless implicit, is that the teacher's learning has ceased at the conclusion of the workshop. The cognitive and logistical burdens that result from attempting to apply a new innovation in the classroom are left unaddressed. Teachers who struggle with an innovation typically muddle through without institutional support or may eventually dilute or abandon the innovation. Yet because the innovation was "taught" in a workshop, the expectation exists that teacher implementation of the new tool or method should be effortless.

In contrast, teacher-centered professional development focuses squarely on the needs of teachers as learners, as practitioners, and as individuals coping with change. The objectives and content of the professional development are grounded in teachers' classroom needs and goals. Each professional-development session focuses on the convergence of the affective, cognitive, and behavioral components of learning. And workshops are supplemented with other professional-development opportunities, such as lesson study, classroom observation and feedback, mentoring, study groups, and in-class assistance, so that, as much as possible, opportunities for teacher learning are differentiated according to teachers' individual needs. Relationship building with and among teachers is a critical component of teacher-centered professional development. Relationship formation with the professional-development facilitator and with colleagues means that teachers are provided with support when wrestling with the difficulties of changing practice. Teachers regarded as learners receive attention to their classroom needs, targeted supports and content to address such needs, and assistance in creating relationships that form the emotional, logistical, and cognitive framework bolstering attempts to improve practice. These integral pieces of teacher-centered professional development may, in turn, support a change toward more collaborative teacher practice.

IDENTIFYING TEACHER NEEDS AND STRENGTHS

What are the key components of teacher-centered professional development, and how can they lead to school-based communities of practice? In the preceding paragraphs, we have identified some core problems: professional development often remains a top-down endeavor, and teacher professional development can be more deficit- than asset-driven, focusing on some perceived quality that teachers lack, as opposed to building on teachers' strengths to help them become more successful. Although district and school goals and exigencies should, in large measure, determine the content and goals of professional development, the main source of information about teachers' professional goals, and the types of professional-development activities that would best help teachers attain these goals, should come from teachers themselves.

This information can be obtained through multiple channels—classroom observations; more traditional information-gathering instruments such as surveys, structured interviews, and focus-group questionnaires; and examinations of teacher work. Self-perception surveys, in which teachers rate their skills in a particular area (for example, computer skills), can often be unreliable owing to difficulty in ascertaining one's level of proficiency in a domain. However, such surveys do provide insight into teachers' level of comfort or confidence with computers, which serve as a metric of teacher attitudes toward technology. This information in turn can help in determining the degree and kind of technology to be used in professional-development sessions and in framing the overarching instructional goal for teacher use of technology.

Needs assessment should not be confined to teacher weaknesses but should include teacher strengths. Teachers can share examples of activities and lesson plans that they feel best reflect their strengths as instructors and that indicate the types of activities they want to build upon, refine, and conduct with students. Elements of these activities can then be woven into the professional-development sessions. Classroom observations also serve to highlight teachers' interpersonal and instructional strengths, enabling these abilities to be incorporated into the sessions. Strong instructional leaders can thus be encouraged to serve as mentors and exemplars for their colleagues, within the actual professional-development activities, in the reflection sessions that follow, and during the course of the school day.

A more valuable, but often overlooked, source of rich information about teacher needs arises through facilitated teacher conversations—meeting with groups of teachers to discuss their goals, fears, and hopes concerning a particular innovation. In the case of computer integration, the authors found that many teachers' fears were related to classroom management, with concerns revolving around a control–chaos axis. In essence, teachers were afraid that the presence of computers in the classroom was distracting and potentially subversive. As teacher fears were probed, three imagined scenarios, each resulting in chaos, loomed large. In one scenario, students would increasingly agitate to use the computers. The teacher would refuse. Eventually, students would become aware of the teacher's lack of expertise with computers. This realization would result in a loss of respect for the teacher and in a breakdown of classroom control.

In the second scenario, students would successfully lobby the teacher to use the classroom computers, but with the same result: students would discover the teacher's lack of familiarity with the technology, and the teacher would lose face and classroom control. The third scenario involved equity of access. The lack of a perfect 1:1 student–computer ratio would necessitate grouping, and this, too, given teacher concerns regarding students' behavioral problems, would result in chaos.

These conversations were invaluable resources and sources of guidance, as they informed the design of activities that focused on building teachers' confidence level with computers while addressing teacher fears involving control; decentralization of authority; student collaboration and noise levels; and classroom management of a limited resource (the computer). This emphasis on the more emotional domains of learning was the intangible that helped teachers change practice.

Such conversations also were essential in the incremental formation of school-based communities of practice. First, they demonstrated to teachers that the professional-development providers were taking their concerns seriously and would address them in professional-development sessions. This was the first step in a relationship between professional-development providers and teachers based on trust and open communication.

Second, in talking with their interviewer (the professional-development provider), teachers were in many cases talking to one another for the first time about their needs and challenges, discovering their common experiences across subject areas and grade levels.

THE ELEMENTS OF LEARNING

Professional development is about learning. Beyond the obvious focus on the cognitive elements of learning (new knowledge and skills), teacher-centered professional development also focuses on affective and behavioral elements of learning. In this case, *affective* refers to how students learn and how teachers build empathy for their students as learners; *behavioral* here refers to how new knowledge and skills translate into new classroom practice. It is this focus not just on what is learned, but on how it is transferred to the classroom, that essentially distinguishes a community of learning from a community of practice. And the focus on sustained teacher *behavioral* change and mutual support for teacher change make the formation of communities of practice more beneficial to schools.

Cognitive Elements of Learning

The best professional development is grounded in evidence-based research on best practices in teaching and learning and provides teachers with opportunities to observe, participate in, discuss, adapt, and apply these practices in their own teaching. In so doing, teachers reflect on their own practice to determine whether their classrooms are conducive to optimal teaching and learning. Accordingly, they begin to make changes to create an atmosphere that best promotes learning.

Teachers, like all learners, come to professional-development sessions with their own mental models and their own prior knowledge, beliefs, and values concerning technology use, instruction, and the role of teachers and students. When teachers engage in team-based activities in which learning occurs as a result of communication, shared meaning-making, and critical reflection, knowledge becomes not only an individual creation, but a collective, consensual construct. Old mental models about technology, curriculum, the nature of learning, and the roles of teachers and students are transformed into new awareness about how individuals learn practices that best promote such learning.

Affective Elements of Learning: Focus on the Teacher as a Learner

To help teachers understand and empathize with the needs of young learners, professional development should immerse teachers in the very types of learning environments envisioned for their own classrooms—in activities that are student-centered, curriculum-based, interdisciplinary in nature, and appropriate to the teachers' level of instruction (elementary, middle, or high school).

In such professional development, the facilitator becomes the teacher, and teachers become the students. In professional development sessions focusing on technology integration to support learner-centered instruction, the facilitator can model setting up a problem- or project-based activity, use collaborative grouping strategies, and employ open-ended questioning techniques and classroom-management strategies. Mindful of teachers' fears about control and chaos, professional-development providers can demonstrate instructional techniques to transform the teacher from a micromanager to a guide and facilitator who accommodates active student learning and "good noise" (conversations about the activity) while keeping students on task and focused and minimizing levels of "bad noise" (conversations that are off task).

Behavioral Elements of Learning: Focus on the Teacher as an Adult Learner

Teacher-centered professional development helps teachers experience different types of learning from the point of view of a younger learner. But it also addresses the needs of teachers as adult learners. Adults often learn best when learning opportunities allow for autonomy and self-direction. Accordingly, adult learners tend to use past experiences to understand new information, to seek out new information as it is needed, and to apply new information to immediate circumstances (Knowles, 1984). Thus, professional development should offer teachers concrete learning experiences, combined with opportunities for reflection to encourage them to form their own beliefs. Further, such skills training for teachers should stimulate and scaffold active experimentation within their own practices (Claxton & Murrell, 1987).

Concentrating on teachers as adult learners also entails focusing on application of new knowledge, skills, and understanding. During each professional-development session, teachers can identify a new activity or approach they will attempt to apply in their classroom in the interim period between professional-development sessions. Professional-development providers, school-based coaches, administrators, and teacher colleagues can assist teachers in this attempt and can also provide a system of monitoring, support, and accountability. Professional-development sessions themselves can and should also be a forum for teachers to apply and share new practices. For example, teachers can be provided with a whole day of collaborative, structured work time and a day when they themselves conduct learner-centered, technology-integrated, interdisciplinary activities in which their peers and professional-development provider participate as active learners and provide critical feedback.

Although research on professional development points to engaging teachers deeply with their content area, the professional development outlined in this book did not address a particular content area. It was multidisciplinary in nature. The activities centered on cultivating certain skills and on learning concepts, rather than on amassing a particular body of knowledge. This approach was deliberately chosen by the professional-development providers. The participating teachers on each campus taught a variety of subjects. By focusing on one particular subject area, at the expense of others, middle and high school teachers would have lost interest in that particular activity and would have been less inclined to work across disciplines.

The interdisciplinary nature of the activities was also designed to compel teachers to think beyond their own areas of expertise. This approach inevitably prompted many instances of cooperation and collaboration, in which teachers began to partner on interdisciplinary activities. For example, teachers invited students from another class to use their classroom's computers or offered to help colleagues and students with a portion of the activity that fell under their content area. Further, as rigid divisions grew more fluid, teachers incorporated practices into their subject area that were more typically associated with a different subject area. For instance, science teachers initiated the use of student journals, and language arts teachers introduced spreadsheets to enumerate and display a literary character's personal traits.

BUILDING RELATIONSHIPS

The glue in community building is relationships with colleagues. Community is about creating and sustaining relationships, and relationships take time to develop and solidify. The isolating structure of many schools—particularly middle and high schools, where teaming may not exist and where teachers are segregated by content area—often impedes the formation of school-based communities.

Long-term and "high touch" professional development involves continuous interaction among the professional-development provider and participating teachers, and provides the supportive structure within which relationships, and eventually community, can take root and thrive. These relationships are critical to the formation of community within schools.

Teacher and Facilitator

An effective model of professional development is to have one person work continuously with a set of teachers over an extended period of time.

By conducting teacher needs assessment and classroom observations, this provider can create learning activities based on teacher needs, as well as provide school-based professional-development activities; frequent, intensive on-site follow-up and coaching; and telephone and e-mail support.

Through such a model, strong professional and personal relationships can emerge between teachers and the professional-development provider. Teachers come to trust the facilitator, to see her as an advocate, and to gradually allow her to become part of their classroom world. The provider, in turn, develops a better understanding of the daily tribulations faced by teachers, of their attempts to balance the demands of teaching with a family life, the challenges of testing, and the requisites of a new type of professional development. This form of professional support—an intensive coaching and mentoring approach—can provide teachers with multiple levels of assistance. According to this model, a colleague may co-teach a difficult concept in the classroom or assist in brainstorming curriculum ideas or projects. More important, by functioning as the teachers' "teacher," the professional developer models an optimal teacher–student relationship emphasizing learning through social interaction.

Between Teachers

In addition to the isolated nature of the teaching profession, the often-taxing nature of working in low-performing schools presents certain barriers that can impede the formation of a supportive and communitarian school-based environment. Low self-esteem; professional isolation; fear of embarrassment or failure; a sense of disconnection from student experiences (especially when those students are of a different racial or ethnic background); pressure to cover the curriculum; and feelings of powerlessness are often felt by teachers in such environments. The challenge for any professional-development provider or change agent is to erode such impediments by helping teachers move from a practice based on isolation and autonomy to one grounded in collaboration. To do this, professional development must emphasize the social nature of learning and the idea of learning as play.

Professional development may work best when it is perceived as neither work nor leisure. Project-based approaches in professional development can create a fun atmosphere that allays teacher fears and invites creativity, allowing for some degree of nonconformity, the expression of individual personalities, and the emergence of a group personality. The authors recall a professional-development activity in which teachers were to sell a car on an Internet used-car lot that they would create. Teachers were sent outside to photograph and inventory a car. Middle-aged, otherwise highly conservative women draped themselves over a pickup truck in the parking lot, in imitation of the classic female prop in automobile advertising. Peals of laughter rang out as they photographed one another in various poses, constructed their humorous Web page car lot, and acted out their team roles as used-car salespeople.

As with young learners, play is a major ingredient in teachers' learning. Play makes professional-development sessions and learning enjoyable, and it provides an impetus for teachers' continued attendance at sessions, particularly if scheduled after school hours. Play also lessens the potential for individual embarrassment, isolation, and failure. As one teacher stated to the authors after two years of professional development, "We learned so much and we had a blast!"

Because individuals generate new knowledge by working together and sharing ideas, teacher-centered professional development uses teams, with discrete roles and responsibilities, as much as possible. Teams allow teachers to get to know and to work with colleagues in other departments and grades. This collaboration leads to informal sharing of professional experiences and expectations; greater personal and professional connections; and a general esprit de corps among teachers. Such connections form the foundation of community. Additionally, assuming a role within a team has important social implications.

The project-based focus, and the assignment of team roles as part of each project, allows teachers to step out of the teacher role and to become the "manager," the "photographer," the "layout editor," the "driver," and so on, within his or her team. This team-based and group-role–based approach can make the learning process less threatening than it might be if the teacher were alone. Within a group setting, teachers feel safe trying something new and making mistakes. This willingness to try and fail lowers inhibitions toward new learning, even if the material might be perceived as difficult. Additionally, group work means that teachers do not need to be in charge of or do everything—just one thing. With teamwork, all individual members' chances for success increase.

The teaming aspect of professional-development activities offers teachers a ready-made model of how to create collaborative groups in their own classrooms, complete with team roles and responsibilities. It showcases strategies for how teachers might promote student cooperation and collaboration and models both the implicit and explicit individual roles and responsibilities that are part of teamwork. Activities illustrate how teachers can set up fun, motivational, engaging instructional activities for students and how they can successfully employ computers in the classroom even when they feel far from competent with a particular piece of software.

Finally, professional development that is grounded in play can foster connections among "head, heart and hands" (Lyons, 1990). Within project-based teams, teachers are not only acquiring new skills, information, and awareness, but also creating actual, tangible computer-based products, of which they are often extremely proud. They receive praise as their team presents a final project, and they thus experience the positive reinforcement and motivator of group acceptance and the sense of satisfaction that comes from human creation.

Through participation in professional development that focuses on learning, ways that teachers learn, and the importance of learning as a collaborative process, teachers recognize that certain practices are not optimal for learning, such as listening to lectures, working in isolation, and the one-size-fits-all approach of everyone doing the same thing at the same time. They experience firsthand that other practices, such as collaborating on an authentic task, are more closely aligned with their own learning. They become aware of what they like and don't like and begin to alter instruction accordingly. In the case of technology, teachers realize that technology and collaboration make learning more fun and that their students are more likely to engage in activities when they enjoy them. As one teacher told the authors and her colleagues: "I am so embarrassed when I think about how I used to teach. But that's what we were told to do." Another teacher remarked, "No wonder my students were bored," as she discussed the difference between her practice at that point and two years earlier. "I'd have been bored, too," she admitted. A third teacher reported, "I've taught for twenty-two years; I learned how to teach in this past year."

REFLECTION

Teachers need opportunities to reflect on the learning they have experienced in professional development. Teacher-centered professional development provides teachers with whole-group, small-group, and individual reflection opportunities in which they discuss their own learning experiences; share new individual understandings of learning, ideas, and concerns; examine what does and does not work in the classroom and why; and formulate shared knowledge experiences. These critical reflection sessions help teachers to plan and work together to adapt and implement strategies that are modeled in the professional-development activities. More important, opportunities for group reflection and dialogue help teachers to develop their own shared instructional philosophy and body of knowledge, which together bolster the community of practice.

SUPPORT

Teachers, like students, need ongoing support. They need time to learn new information, then apply and revise it in their classrooms. They need support and pressure from administrators to implement the desired objectives of professional development. They need permission to take risks—and to fail, and to learn from their mistakes. Professional development that is truly teacher centered provides teachers with time, support, guidance, and in-class assistance to help them implement and apply new instructional strategies in their own classrooms and to learn, in turn, how they can become supportive mentors, peers, and coaches to their colleagues and to their students in the learning process.

CONCLUSION

Human beings are by nature learners, and learning is critical to people's sense of personal and professional well-being. High-quality professional development is grounded in the belief that teachers are learners and are motivated by a desire to improve their practice and to better serve students. Professional development that is truly teacher centered meets the following conditions:

- It is based not just on empirical data but on teachers' needs, goals, fears, and hopes.
- It is long-term and focuses on teacher learning and teacher practice.
- It provides the social context for professional learning and relationship building with the same cohort of people over an extended time period.
- It helps teachers understand the affective, behavioral, and cognitive dimensions of learning.
- It promotes open, honest reflection and self-examination.
- It provides teachers with the time, resources, and support to work together to improve their practice.

Professional development that follows these guidelines can result in new classroom practices and communities to support those practices.

3

Technology: A Catalyst
for Change

Community is born of conflict, not consensus.

—Edward Stennet

Can technology help to create communities of practice? Given the plentiful research and anecdotes related to technology and community formation, the answer seems to be that it can. Yet most case studies and examples of technology and community formation document the communicative power of computers to bring people together across distances, as in online communities.

In contrast, this chapter examines the role of technology as a catalyst for the creation of groups not separated by distances—in the form of communities of practice located in the same school building. In this case, it is not the communicative power of technology that brings people together. Rather, through developing an understanding of how to teach with technology, teachers re-imagine themselves as learners and reach out to their peers and to their students to give and receive support in a cooperative learning endeavor.

To unleash technology's potential to support community formation, attention must be paid to the nature of professional development offered to teachers. The training should closely match teachers' needs, emphasize their comfort with technology, and empower them to use technology as one of many tools in the classroom. Unfortunately, the technology skills training offered to teachers often lacks these qualities.

SKILLS TRAINING: A STRONG TREATMENT?

The rhetoric surrounding the transformational powers of technology, particularly in the early stages of its introduction into U.S. schools, portrayed computers as possessing an almost intrinsic ability to improve student learning, create collaborative professional communities, inculcate higher-order thinking skills, and reform instruction. This view of computers as a "strong treatment" for what ailed instruction, teacher performance, and student achievement often resulted in an inordinate and unnecessary focus on skills training, the underlying idea of which seemed to be that if a teacher could master computer operations, transformation of the learning process would follow.

Despite substantive technology-skills training, however, many teachers still approach technology with great trepidation. Skills training often does not result in altered instructional practice. This gap between skills acquisition and classroom use occurs because of three weaknesses in skills-based technology instruction. First, despite inevitable focus on the creation of an academic product (e.g., using PowerPoint to present a lesson) within typical professional-development sessions, technology remains the primary focus, with curriculum as a secondary focus. Such training casts technology and curriculum as separate entities in teachers' minds and makes technology manipulation appear all the more important.

Second, skills training has the unanticipated consequence of convincing teachers that they must be experts in the operation of technology, in troubleshooting technical issues, and in instructional implications. Because they believe they lack this expertise, teachers may avoid technology use altogether. Finally, the intensive length of some of these training sessions, in most cases three to six hours per application, has left many teachers with the belief that they would need to devote a similar portion of curriculum time to train students in the use of technology, yet such long blocks of instructional time are unavailable. Fortunately, by rethinking the way teachers learn to use technology, these sorts of problems and misperceptions can be avoided.

Beyond Skills Training: The 5J Approach

If technology is used as an instructional tool, embedded within strong instructional techniques, and tied to curricular goals, it can promote better instruction and greater student collaboration, enhancing student learning. However—and perhaps unexpectedly—professional development must promote both technology integration and learning by actually *minimizing* the importance of computers within professional development.

The 5J approach, as we have labeled it, ensures that all technology instruction within each professional development activity has the following characteristics:

- **Job-related:** Focused on classroom (i.e., instructional and curricular) needs
- **Just enough:** Emphasizing increased comfort, not proficiency, with computers
- **Just in time:** Providing teachers with skills as needed and focused on using only the tools they have at their immediate disposal
- **Just in case:** Encouraging teachers to plan sufficiently in the event of a computer malfunction
- **Just try it:** Applying enough pressure and support to impel teachers to use computers in their classrooms

The following paragraphs describe the elements of this approach in greater detail.

Job-related

The job-relatedness aspect of the 5J approach means that, unlike normal skills-training sessions, which treat computer use as an end in itself, a systems approach to computers is applied to professional development. Within such an approach, the classroom is the "system" and the computer simply one component of the system—one that supports learning by allowing work to be accomplished more efficiently, or by allowing students to organize, analyze, or communicate information; create a product; or collaborate with peers.

Thus computers are viewed not as an end in themselves, but as a way to improve the components within the classroom system—composed of teacher, instruction, assessment, curriculum, and student learning. The focus of the activities is not on a software tool, but on an instructional method, a certain problem- or project-based approach, or a particular classroom-management strategy.

As a tool, the computer is dynamic; its function is not static but constantly changes in response to specific instructional needs. For example, teachers can choose the software that best allows them to carry out a project and complete a final product. Teachers certainly gain mechanical and procedural knowledge about computers, but the focus is really on the generative powers of computers—how computers, when used appropriately, can generate new knowledge and ideas, allow for innovative expression of such ideas, and promote collaboration.

No activity is conducted for the sake of teachers learning, for example, spreadsheets or presentation software. Rather, the goal is to understand how computers can best be employed as a tool for knowledge generation, communication, analysis, and self-expression. In this approach, professional-development activities may not even employ computers, or may use them along with other learning tools, such as books, maps, art supplies, calculators, markers, and chart paper. In other words, computers are considered one tool among many that may be used to promote learning.

Just Enough

The focus in this model of professional development is not on proficiency with technology, but on comfort in embedding technology within a curriculum activity. Teachers are expected to cultivate a minimal set of technology skills—"just enough" to create a product or solve a problem.

A typical activity involves showing one teacher from each collaborative group no more than five commands for using a piece of software and sending that person back to teach the rest of the group. When teachers encounter challenges in using software, facilitators encourage intra-group or inter-group problem solving, consultation of cheat sheets, or use of the software's help menu. Only when all collaborative options are exhausted do facilitators intercede, and then only in a hands-off fashion, providing oral guidance but never removing the mouse or keyboard from a teacher's control. Not surprisingly, this is initially a quite unpopular strategy, with grumbling from many anxious novice users who are used to being "given a fish," versus figuring out what to do with the rod. For facilitators, it is often difficult *not* to intercede when teachers are visibly struggling and exhorting the facilitator to save them from their technology frustrations.

The principle of "just enough" extends beyond software instruction to encompass hardware access. Teachers often believe that more is better—that more technology in a classroom will yield a more learner-centered environment and that hardware limitations will prevent the creation of such an environment. Limited hardware is cited by teachers as a rationale for not attempting more collaborative approaches. Statements such as "I have one computer and twenty-five students"; "I have thirty kids and only four computers"; and "If I only had more computers" are familiar refrains.

To address these hardware constraints, professional-development sessions should employ the same ratio of learners to computers (1:25 or 1:4) that teachers face in their own classrooms, focusing on activities that emphasize collaboration, negotiation, and sharing of one resource (the computer). Such a grouping strategy demonstrates to teachers that scarcity of resources can actually breed, not impede, collaboration and that innovation does not always depend on resources.

Just in Time

Similar to the idea of "just enough," professional development should support teachers' learning "just in time"—that is, when they are ready to learn. Facilitators must constantly question teachers to identify learning goals and needs to be addressed over the course of professional-development sessions. Once topics are identified, sessions can be developed to help teachers learn those skills and practices as the need for them arises.

In addition, using the technology available at the teachers' schools is crucial. Otherwise, technology learning cannot be applied in a timely manner. Whether teachers have access to Microsoft-, Linux-, or Apple-based products, professional development should be designed such that these software tools are used during the sessions. In this way, teachers can take what is learned in the sessions and immediately apply it in their classrooms. Teachers should never be provided instruction on platforms that they do not use, nor should instruction employ software that teachers do not have unless the school can provide for its immediate purchase.

Another critical element provided just in time is follow-up support. A facilitator or site coordinator should frequently check in with teachers to ascertain what assistance they need regarding technology use and learner-centered practices in their classrooms. Additional assistance with lesson planning or software must be available at the point in time when teachers are ready to approach those subjects. Monthly follow-up sessions that coincide with a particular project teachers might have scheduled are needed to provide timely assistance.

Just in Case

Before professional-development activities, teachers should be asked to describe their fears regarding technology. As mentioned earlier, teachers commonly express concern about classroom management of limited hardware resources. How can they use technology when they have only one, two, or four computers and twenty-five to thirty-five students? They also worry what to do if computers break down. And what if students cannot use or easily learn the software in question, particularly if the teacher also feels uncomfortable with the software?

These concerns reflect larger fears about control. Technology threatens to disrupt classroom equilibrium based on teacher control and expertise in all matters. Limited hardware necessitates grouping, making it harder for teachers to control the class in general and unruly students in particular.

Inability to help students with software or to troubleshoot a computer problem might reveal teachers to be less than omniscient. Teachers fear chaos will ensue.

Professional development can help teachers address these control issues by adopting a "just in case" attitude toward computers that emphasizes careful planning of the classroom activity. By viewing computers as one in a suite of learning tools, teachers reduce their chances of being unprepared if a computer fails or if a collaborative computer-based activity falls flat. Through deliberate grouping of students with varying technical expertise, teachers can delegate computer training to students, thus freeing themselves from this burden and shifting some control to students. And by employing several tools, both "high-tech" and "low-tech," teachers can gauge whether and how computers make a difference in student learning. Based on that knowledge, they can make better decisions about when technology might help them do something more effectively or help students learn.

This just-in-case approach forces teachers to plan and organize instruction in a more detailed and comprehensive fashion than might be required if computers were not part of the activity. By thinking through and planning for all contingencies, teachers can better prepare and organize instruction.

Just Try It

Central to change and to the formation of any community of practice are the concepts of action and changing practice. The expectation must be clear that after every single professional-development session, teachers will return to their classrooms, use a new instructional approach and technology there, and report the results to colleagues and the facilitator. In this model, teachers are not expected to produce specific results by using technology; they are, however, expected to implement what they have learned. As such, when everyone "just tries" technology, its implementation becomes a work in progress that by its very nature requires collaboration among teachers.

Three strategies help to ensure that teachers "just try" technology. One is to deemphasize the importance of teachers' expertise with software and hardware. Instead, teachers are encouraged to envision themselves as project managers who set up the activity, with students as team members who carry out the technical part. A second strategy is to provide teachers with follow-up support and to encourage peer support. The final strategy is to solicit the input of two groups typically overlooked in professional development and not thought of as change agents—novice teachers and resistors.

In large-group discussions, the input of the so-called experts or leaders should be considered important, but the viewpoints and reservations of novice and so-called resistant teachers must be valued, as well. Both groups should be encouraged to share their fears, frustrations, and reservations without censure or disapprobation. Novice teachers help to remind more experienced colleagues that classroom management, good organization and planning, and communication skills are critical to the successful implementation of learner-centered, technology-integrated approaches. Resistors can articulate fundamental, though often hidden or embedded, teacher beliefs, and their statements can reveal school-based dichotomies and inconsistencies that could undermine optimal computer use or even erode the types of learning environments the school outwardly advocates. Facilitators can show empathy in response to such teachers' concerns and fears, meanwhile emphasizing a just-try-it approach that encourages their colleagues to exhort and invite these frightened or resistant teachers to collaborate in a small technology-integrated activity or, even more simply, to allow students to use a particular piece of hardware or software in a particular activity.

TRANSFORMING TEACHING AND LEARNING

Cumulatively, this 5J approach can result in the transformation not only of instruction within classrooms, but of student-to-student interactions, teacher–student relationships, and teacher collaboration. With the 5J method, classroom use of technology can expand greatly even when past efforts have fallen short. Student and teacher roles can shift in ways that empower students, including students for whom teachers hold low expectations.

Increased Use

We found that teachers' overall regular use of instructional technology soared from 17 percent before 5J-based professional development (and after hours of skills training) to 80 percent after two years. Further, regular classroom use of instructional technology by application increased dramatically—in some cases tripling (as in the case of spreadsheets) or increasing twenty-five-fold (in the case of electronic presentation software).

Two important characteristics of the 5J approach supported this rapid technology adoption. First, the 5J approach fast-tracked teachers in the process of knowledge acquisition from the *cognitive* stage of computer learning—which focused on skills acquisition, a hallmark of technology training—to the *associative* stage, in which they could apply a skill directly without first having to think through how to do so, and then to the *autonomous* stage of computer learning, when skills had become so automated that application of skill required minimal cognitive involvement (Anderson, 1995).

Second, the 5J approach integrated computers more easily and rapidly into the existing classroom environment. Rogers (1995) has identified five criteria that affect the rate of adoption of a particular innovation. They are *relative advantage* (helping the adopter to do something better); *compatibility* (with the needs and experiences of the adopter); a lack of *complexity*; *trialability* (the degree to which there is opportunity to experiment and practice with the equipment); and *observability* (meaning teachers can observe the innovation's use). The 5J approach maps well with such a framework. It focuses on and models technology's compatibility with both curriculum and instruction and demonstrates how, when used properly, technology can improve instruction. Professional-development sessions stress the simplicity of computer use and allow teachers to experiment with computers.

Because, in this approach, exposure to technology is embedded within inquiry-based, collaborative activities that promote higher-order skills and engage the session facilitator as a guide and the teachers as active learners, teachers can import session content wholesale and adapt it to particular content areas. For the most part, teachers become exemplary users of technology—more reflective and less reflexive about when, how, and why to employ computers in the classroom. They learn to use technology not for technology's sake, but because it can help students to do something better or allow them to do something that was otherwise impossible. In our experience, teachers integrated computer use within project-based, collaborative activities, created computer-based projects of increasing cognitive complexity, and permitted students greater autonomy in the design of their technology-based classroom products.

This increased use of instructional technology, coupled with a continued emphasis on the model of "just enough"—that is, minimal skills cultivation—facilitates teachers' shift toward technology-integrated, learner-centered approaches. Comfort with technology takes precedence over technology expertise, with the result that teachers allow students to use a technology application even when the teachers themselves have not mastered the application. Technology comfort invalidates the old belief that teachers cannot use computers until they are experts.

Teachers also recognize that a small amount of input (their technical knowledge) can result in increased output (students' improved work using technology tools). Consequently, teachers become more comfortable in allowing students to teach one another and, in time, the teachers themselves in software use. Indeed, teachers may first cede some control to students in the area of technology and subsequently begin to see students as coequal, or even superior, in technology knowledge. Often, teachers are surprised at students' facility. Gradually, they begin to accord students more control and autonomy in research and expression than would be the case were the technology not available.

Changed Roles

This gradual decentralization of authority where technology is concerned may extend to other areas. As students prove themselves competent with computers, and as their levels of engagement and the quality of their work begins to improve on tasks involving computer use in the classroom, teachers begin to decentralize control in other domains, such as by giving students a choice of final products, allowing them to work at their own pace on an activity, and letting them venture beyond the classroom for research and communication purposes.

Another role-changing aspect of technology lies in what typically is viewed as a problem: limited hardware. In promoting student collaboration, less has proven to be more. Since no classroom, with the exception of labs, enjoys a perfect student–computer ratio, teachers must group students in order to take advantage of technology. To allow for such groupings, both the physical and organizational landscapes of the classroom become less centralized. Students work together and rely on one another—as opposed to the teacher—for guidance and creative input. Within this dynamic, the teacher becomes more of a facilitator. As with the changes that arise when teachers cede some control to students in response to the implementation of technology, the shift that results from work being accomplished in groups can lead many teachers to restructure curricula to allow for greater technology use and student activity.

Changed Expectations

In schools whose students are low-income and/or ethnically diverse, many teachers expect little in the way of academic excellence. However, when students' use of technology allows them to demonstrate that they are capable, teachers gain confidence in allowing them greater autonomy, which in turn may result in improved student performance. "I had no idea that he knew so much about history—and computers," one social studies teacher commented after observing a particular low-achieving student use technology to create a Revolutionary War concept map.

Classrooms (labs) with a one-to-one student–computer ratio often exhibit a lower degree of learner-centered approaches. In these classrooms, students do not interact with one another but with the technology, even when students are supposed to be collaborating on an activity. There is a greater tendency for low group cohesion, with individuals retreating to their individual computers and working independently. In these classrooms, we have found that technology functions as a tool for individualized instruction, not for shared learning. Computer labs stand in stark contrast with the community-building effects of technology that is introduced as a new tool in the regular classroom setting.

THE EMERGENCE OF COMMUNITIES OF PRACTICE

As expressed in the quotation that heads this chapter, teacher community formation is born not of acceptance of a new and imposing innovation, but of conflict with this innovation. This conflict centers on several areas: the necessity of learning something new, hardware limitations, lack of software and hardware skills, the decentralization of classroom authority, and the complexity that computers add to the instructional process. By addressing and surmounting these conflicts in cooperation with their peers, teachers can build school-based communities of practice.

New Learning

Technology can be the catalyst for teachers re-imagining themselves as co-learners with colleagues and students. Although technology is not the main course in the 5J professional-development approach, it is the main ingredient used in most activities. Its strength as a treatment does not rest in its instrumentality—its capacity to glean information instantly, to problem solve, or to communicate. Rather, technology's strength lies in its service as a method of "learning about learning." When used as a meaningful tool within a certain professional-development framework, technology becomes a mirror that allows teachers to reflect on best practices for learning and for instruction.

In becoming aware of the optimal approaches for their own learning, teachers begin to see commonalities between their needs as learners and those of their students. Sometimes teachers' technology learning experiences produce discomfort that gives them insight into students' needs. Consider the following statement from a teacher who experienced firsthand how a computer lab setting can alienate students: "Last year, we would all sit in a lab and follow [the trainer]. I immediately got lost but he never said we could work together, so I didn't want to bother anyone. I just turned into one of the kids; I tuned out and played Solitaire [on the PC] for the rest of the day."

Other teachers commented on best approaches to learning how to learn. One reported: "What was so wonderful about the sessions was that they were so hands-on. We were just like the kids. They gave us a problem and we had to figure it out. We had to work together as a group to figure it out. We learned how to use the technology together and we had a blast."

Another teacher reached similar conclusions and also became aware of potential pitfalls: "The facilitators put us in the role of students. And we experienced the same frustrations as the kids, so we learned what to do and not do with our students." A third teacher discovered how it feels to be rushed by an instructor: "We could work together on the computer. We didn't have to work alone. And we had time to figure things out. . . . Now I know we don't give kids enough time to figure things out. We expect them to get it right away when we don't get it right away."

Hardware Limitations

The lack of a perfect student–computer ratio presents significant logistical burdens to teachers. As resourceful professionals, teachers can band together to overcome this impediment by leveraging hardware resources across classrooms. The concept of "the classroom" becomes less fixed and more fluid as teachers coordinate schedules to allow one teacher to send students to another classroom where computers are not in use. This interclassroom cooperation may broaden to collaboration. We found that teachers realized that they could offset hardware constraints by engaging with colleagues in interdisciplinary activities in which one classroom used computers while the others did not, or in which certain groups of students fanned out to use the computers in participating classrooms. This cooperation and collaboration, albeit initiated by technology, ultimately brings teachers together and focuses them on the critical elements of curriculum, content, and instruction.

Skills Limitations

Feelings of uncertainty about technology, and of inadequacy in using it, are a source of anxiety for teachers. The 5J approach to learning how to integrate technology can shift reliance from external experts (facilitators) to in-house expertise (other teachers). Peer assistance becomes an increasing source of additional support as teachers move from private practice, to learning communities, to communities of practice. As one teacher reported, "We'd help each other with the technology. Everyone would check up on each other and see if they needed help with anything, and we knew who was really good with a piece of software and [would] have them teach us what they knew." Another stated, "Going through this to-gether, made us [the faculty] even closer because we were all in the same boat with the computers." This sharing of expertise may then diversify from technology to other domains—including curriculum, instruction, and classroom management—as teachers begin to leverage knowledge across a range of areas.

Shared Expertise

This mutual aid around computer operations helps shift knowledge from the private to the public realm and diffuses knowledge across the spectrum of teachers, from the innovators and leaders to the late adopters and resistors. It fosters a culture of inquiry and learning—meaning it is okay, even desirable, to ask questions, seek additional help, and become a continual learner. It creates knowledge dissemination networks. Teachers share existing knowledge of print and Web resources, trial versions of software, and established mechanisms to generate new knowledge. For example, teachers can establish student "tech squads" to help colleagues who are having difficulty or who did not participate in the professional development. They can hold after-school sessions for one another and disseminate technology tips.

More important are the emotional bonds that result from this mutual support. The sharing of expertise about technology creates a culture of reciprocity. Teachers help one another knowing and expecting that they in turn will receive help when they need it. This expectation of mutual assistance creates a sense of collegiality and trust among teachers who previously had little contact or interaction with one another. By asking for help, teachers show healthy professional vulnerability, knowing that they can trust colleagues.

Added Complexity

To fully capitalize on the potential of computers, instructional practices need to change. Curriculum suddenly becomes more complex and less linear. Content suddenly seems more infinite, interactive, and open to interpretation. The Internet and CD-ROM encyclopedias can displace the teacher as the intellectual authority. Teachers cannot maintain whole-class instruction using one, two, or four computers.

The presence of technology can cause teachers cognitive, logistical, and in many cases emotional disequilibrium. This discomfort pushes teachers to reach out to one another for support and assistance—after all, other faculty members are experiencing the same situation. Within the professional-development sessions, after school, and during planning periods, teachers meet to relearn how to teach with this new technology. Learning moves to practice as they begin to plan activities together, experiment, innovate, and reflect on new paradigms of instruction. By increasingly helping one another in their classrooms, team-teaching and collaborating on interdisciplinary activities, teachers develop a shared practice and a culture of experimentation in which it is okay to try and to fail, to learn from mistakes, and to constantly revise practice.

The power of computers to promote community building does not rest with computers' innate capabilities. Community formation, like instructional improvement, results from practitioners' cognitive and emotional conflict with this new tool and from their subsequent coming together, learning together, and working together to overcome fears and to harness technology's potential to improve their professional practice.

4

From Old Guard to Vanguard: Veteran Teachers as Leaders of Communities of Practice

I can't imagine how I taught before. I think back to my old teaching and think, "God, how boring!" I would not want to have been in my class. It was awful. Now I see [students] interacting with each other and just learning and not worrying, "Is this graded? Is this a test? Is this important?" Now they just do the work and they're not worried about grades. They just want to do their best.

—Seventh-grade teacher, Lafitte Middle School

Veteran teachers are not usually associated with innovation and receptivity to new ideas. Instead, they are often seen as impediments to change. This chapter tells the story of how a group of veteran teachers at Lafitte Middle School in Louisiana,[1] in the absence of formal administrative leadership, embraced the use of technology to reorganize teaching, learning, and professional relationships with their students and with one another.

These veteran teachers' enthusiasm was not always so evident. In an initial orientation with teacher volunteers in which the technology-based professional development was introduced, veteran teachers openly expressed their anxiety about technology, their suspicion of innovation, and their belief that professional development was irrelevant to their classroom needs. They stated bluntly that computer technology and learner-centered strategies were just the latest educational fads imposed by a central office with no understanding of teachers' classroom realities. This fad would be replaced with another onerous and ineffective innovation, and so on. In the battle between educational faddism and fundamentalism—that is, hewing to tried-and-true practices—Lafitte teachers revealed themselves that first day as fundamentalists.

Yet at this same orientation meeting, the chorus of skepticism and resistance was interrupted by a gruff dissenting voice. "I don't know about the rest of you, but we're getting computers next year and I want someone to help me teach with them. So I think we might want to quit complaining and take advantage of this."

Louise Boudreau, a sixteen-year veteran, clearly commanded the faculty's respect. After her comment, teacher attitudes perceptibly changed. "I'd like help," admitted one teacher after a few minutes. "All of us language arts teachers will have four computers next year," said another. "We're going to *have* to learn how to use them." Eventually, twenty-five teachers agreed to participate in the project. Louise Boudreau's name was first on the sign-up list.

DIAGNOSING TEACHER NEEDS

Classroom observations of Lafitte's twenty-five teacher participants revealed one dominant instructional style—the teacher as actor and the student as a sort of disinterested and uninterested spectator. In twenty-one of twenty-five classrooms, teachers prompted students for short or rote answers and students sat in rows working wordlessly. In many classrooms, computers functioned as the corpse at a wake, still and silent, covered by sheets, with activity going on despite their presence—except that corpses have previously possessed life, and many of these machines had never even been turned on. One teacher explained that the computers were covered so students wouldn't "break" them. In the limited instances in which computers were employed beyond computer science class, their use was limited to skill-and-drill software.

The intellectual and emotional distance between teachers and students was palpable. There was no sense of connectedness among any of the classroom elements—between students and computers, among students, or between students and teachers. Implementing technology in a meaningful way at Lafitte promised to be a tough task. Teachers needed help with instruction, with technology use, with classroom management, with the disconnect between teaching and learning. But most of all they seemed to need help with job satisfaction.

YEAR ONE: FROM OLD GUARD TO VANGUARD

Lafitte's journey toward change did not follow a straight path. During the initial two days of professional development, teachers proved enthusiastic enough about the activities in which they were engaged. They enjoyed going outdoors in teams to gather data about their community, loved learning how to use a digital camera, and marveled at learning stations (used commonly in elementary school but new to secondary-school teachers), through which they rotated in teams. There were, however, several red flags regarding expected technology implementation. First, many teachers complained about the focus on curriculum and integration at the expense of skills training. They wanted to be led "step by step," they said, through technology instruction in a lab, not shown its use in a classroom setting. Several teachers noted that they could not use software with their students until they became "expert" with it themselves.

During the reflection session at the end of the first day, when asked to share how they might conduct similar activities with their students, several responded, "Oh, I would *never* do this with my students." The lack of a one-to-one ratio between students and computers would necessitate grouping, resulting in "chaos." Teachers said *"they"* (the students) would break the computers. *"They* would go wild if we had activities like this." *"They* would not behave during such activities." *"They* need discipline." Finally, teachers remarked that technology integration and learner-centered approaches could work only in honors classes, because honors students had the requisite skills and work ethic. Louise stated that she would not give up control of her class, as this learner-centered approach demanded. Her complete control of her students made her a good teacher. Her colleagues nodded vigorously in agreement.

At the end of these first two professional-development days, teachers were asked to write a letter of intended practice in which they promised to try one new approach in their classrooms before the next professional-development session. It could be anything—letting students use Power-Point or putting students in groups. The letter of intended practice served as a useful tool through which the professional-development provider and teachers could discuss by e-mail and phone the teachers' intended approach and their fears and logistical needs concerning such a strategy.

Session three began, as all sessions did, with a sharing component. Astonishingly, given the reserve with which the first two professional-development days ended, teachers were experimenting. Several brought examples of students' computer work. Although most of the projects consisted of heavily animated PowerPoint presentations, it was a start, and it showed that teachers were letting students get their hands on the computers. Several more teachers shared stories about successful grouping strategies, which, although rough, did not result in a complete breakdown in classroom order. Instead, teachers observed, students seemed to *like* working in groups and did better work. The teachers seemed genuinely pleased by students' behavioral and cognitive responses to using computers or to working cooperatively. And the teachers themselves delighted in their own and in their colleagues' successes.

In this session, two dynamics emerged that remained constant during the next two years and served as the impetus for change at a campus level. In the first dynamic, teachers' willingness to try something new typically resulted in some degree of success and a higher degree of self-satisfaction, and it changed teachers' perceptions of students, fellow teachers, and themselves. In turn, these altered perceptions formed the rudiments of emergent relationships and eventually led to the formation of a community of practice. The second dynamic was that the change agents at this school were not younger practitioners, but veteran teachers: the "old dogs," as some of them called themselves. These change agents also formed the nucleus of what was to become a community of practice.

Changing Teacher Expectations

If teachers wanted to attempt new classroom approaches—and they did throughout year one—they generally could not confine such approaches to Lafitte's honors students. There simply were not enough of those students. Although some teachers did indeed limit their innovations to their honors classes, many others, who did not teach such classes, attempted new approaches with their "regular" students and were pleased with the results. What seemed to motivate teachers was the success that the "bad" students (and there were many, according to teachers) exhibited through more collaborative and technology-based projects. Beginning in session three and continuing over the next two years, teachers often exclaimed in awe and disbelief: "[So and so] did *that?!*" Teachers began to think, "If this kid can do such a good job in *her* class, then he [or she] can do it in mine."

As in any profession, teachers had created an internal professional hierarchy of who were "good," "bad," and "middling" practitioners, along with a sense of where they themselves fell in the hierarchy. When a teacher who was not considered "good" demonstrated a tangible example of high-quality student work or shared a success story, teachers had thoughts such as: "If she can do such a good job, then I, who am a much better teacher, can do an even better job."[2]

Cumulatively, such trends resulted in a changing constellation of perceptions and fostered the formation of new professional relationships that gradually coalesced into a community. When teachers saw that their "bad" students actually could do good work, formerly poor learners transformed into good ones, and teachers' perception of and relationships with certain students changed. Also, teachers' success with such normally recalcitrant students—and fellow teachers' approbation when they shared their success—gave them feelings of pride and gratification. Teachers began to see certain colleagues as worthy of emulation or as professional peers from whom they could learn, and certain teachers who had always gone unrecognized received positive attention. New leaders began to emerge from teacher ranks. As existing perceptions and mental models were modified or supplanted by evolving expectations and information, instruction moved from an individual, private classroom matter to one based on collective discourse and common celebration. Teaching became a public activity.

Progress Continues

Evidence of teacher enthusiasm and instructional change continued unabated throughout the first year. Monthly follow-up visits were spent helping teachers learn a certain piece of software, reviewing previously learned software, or observing their classes in order to provide feedback on instruction or a specific activity, or help with a particular student's behavior.

During the course of the school year, teachers attempted activities they never would have dared to undertake a year before. For example, several teachers had rearranged their classroom from rows into five learning stations of five students per team to allow students to work together. Each station lasted an entire period, and on the following day each team rotated to a new station (the computer formed one of these stations), so that by week's end all students had completed the same set of activities, but with a greater degree of autonomy. Other teachers, to ensure computer accessibility and equity yet relieve themselves of the stress of micromanaging such access, created sign-in sheets through which students were responsible for assuring and monitoring their own computer time.

By the end of the first year, every classroom but one employed some degree of either technology or student-centered approaches. Often the technology use or the new approaches were rudimentary, but they certainly represented progress, given the absence of either a year earlier.

And although in some instances only nominal progress was made, some classrooms were extraordinary. Loretta, a sixteen-year language arts veteran, struggled for most of the first year with "letting go," and she finally did so in a big way. To accommodate a learner-centered environment, Loretta physically redesigned her classroom with beanbag chairs for a reading corner and the construction of a readers' theater. The level of activity had changed dramatically since the previous year. Before, Loretta was a woman who yelled at and scolded her students. Yet now, Loretta was the model of a guide and facilitator. In one corner of the room, students sprawled comfortably on beanbags, reading silently. In another, a group of students practiced a puppet show of one of Aesop's fables, which they also directed and produced. One student was teaching a group of students how to use the scanner and the software program Print

Shop. Another small group was engaged in a computer grammar game, while a group of three boys were writing a story in a software program Loretta had purchased with her own money.

Students' views of Loretta were positive. "Mrs. Saulnier always does interesting, active, artistic stuff. It's really fun." Loretta was effusive about her new way of teaching, stating that she and her students were "finally enjoying [them]selves."

Indeed, more teachers appeared to be enjoying themselves as they moved away from the front of the classroom. Another language arts teacher, a fifteen-year veteran, regularly sat with students as they did their work. A year before, she had scowled her way through the class period. She agreed that she was happier now using a new mode of instruction. "Since I've changed the way I teach, I love my job. The kids are learning and having a really good time and so am I."

Technology: Old Dogs and New Tricks

Despite these instructional successes, technology was still a wall between veteran and novice faculty, not just in terms of manipulation of software, but in terms of instructional ethos and curriculum integration. Younger teachers, by virtue of their age or their more recent computer training at university, were more comfortable with computers. They were the vanguard. For veteran teachers, though, who had been "paper trained," computers caused worry and consternation. These teachers were the old guard.

Even so, despite this lack of familiarity with technology, or perhaps because of it, the veterans did not use technology for technology's sake, or for reward or remediation, as did many of the novice teachers. In veterans' classrooms, computers became a cognitive tool. Because their technology skills were weaker, these teachers embedded computer use in the curriculum—for example, by having students use the computers to write a report or to create a spreadsheet showing data analysis. The more experienced teachers integrated computers into the classroom in more learner-centered ways than did their novice colleagues: encouraging students to learn from one another; acting as co-learners with students; refraining from taking over the mouse and keyboard and fixing a computer problem for a student; and providing students with substantial freedom in the creation of their computer-based projects.

For example, Louise's language arts class now functioned as two alternating halves. One half of the class worked on small-group activities or with their teacher as needed, while the other half worked in teams at four computers making presentations on their careers units. Louise acted as a learner with students. If someone did something new, she'd ask that student to explain his or her action to the teacher and the other students. She enlisted students to teach one another; indeed, one girl seemed to be the technology consultant for the whole group. After school, Louise even employed her own student technology tutors—students who volunteered to help her improve her skills.

By the end of the first year, teachers were comfortable enough with technology that when asked what they wanted to focus on in the following year's sessions, a group of vocal veteran teachers requested activities that employed team-teaching and interdisciplinary approaches. When pressed about their earlier anxiety about learning as much technology as possible, they responded that now they felt they could learn any type of software. They had enjoyed working in teams and on the interdisciplinary professional-development activities, but now they needed to learn how to implement these approaches in their classrooms.

YEAR TWO: FUNDAMENTALISM AND COMMUNITY

Before the start of the second year of the professional development, however, Lafitte lost its supportive administrators. They were replaced by a principal and vice principal who immediately made it known that Lafitte's emphasis would be on improving test scores—on "back to basics." In another blow to the school, the district was rezoned and Lafitte lost many of the newest teachers, including three of its strongest in technology skills. A majority of its honors students were reassigned to other schools. Finally, the school learned that, once again, not enough of its students had passed the state assessment.

Together, these changes threatened the success and the very survival of the emerging practices and use of technology. If teachers were pressured into a back-to-basics approach, with its focus on "coverage" and rote learning, where would they find time for learner-centered approaches? With even fewer honors students, would the teachers who had restricted learner-centered approaches and technology integration to their honors classes simply decline to attempt any such innovations with remaining students? Would an even larger percentage of non-honors students mean an even greater emphasis on remediation at the expense of more active pedagogical approaches?

The new administrators had inherited a project in which they had little interest or investment. Their reality involved state-mandated test scores. In their view, if computers were to be used, they had to be used to improve those scores: "We really must stress the basics, over and over," intoned the vice principal. Teachers recounted the pressure they felt to go back to "old ways" of instruction.

Despite these mandates, professional-development sessions continued as in year one, but they now reflected teachers' higher-level approaches to both instruction and technology use. Teachers were introduced to problem-based scenarios in which they had to resolve an ill-structured real-world problem, such as increasing population demands for housing versus a desire to preserve a community's green space. In doing this, they used more complex computer tools, including spreadsheets, graphing calculators, and Geographic Information Systems (GIS) viewers. In follow-up sessions, teachers asked less often about technology help and more frequently requested instructional guidance.

Professional-development sessions also provided a forum for teachers to discuss the pressure they felt from administrators and to offer one another emotional and procedural supports. Having seen the positive changes in their classrooms as a result of adopting technology and learner-centered approaches, teachers were quite supportive of the "new ways." Despite administrative pressures, teachers continued to build on the previous year's successes. Computer use continued to evolve. Although "show and tell" applications such as PowerPoint continued to predominate, software use diversified into applications such as spreadsheet, Web-editing, and concept-mapping software, and new tools such as graphing calculators were introduced.

More striking in year two was the degree of collaboration among teachers and students. Whereas classroom activities in the previous year had tended to be cooperative and focused on a single content area, activities during year two became more collaborative. For example, a group of teachers from three grades and several disciplines embarked on an interdisciplinary study of the story "Sadako and the Thousand Paper Cranes." Another group of history and language arts teachers collaborated on the production of a reader's theater—complete with historical scripts, costumes, stage, and scenery—that portrayed characters of the U.S. Civil War.

The trajectory of teacher relationships had evolved from communication to cooperation to eventual collaboration. Simply talking about ideas with others helped teachers, as one teacher attested. "I feel better now, and as I talk to other teachers, asking questions and sharing experiences, it makes me feel more open-minded, and willing to try new things." Communication among teachers appeared to give rise to positive shifts in teachers' instructional practices, as marked changes in pedagogy were noted among teachers who communicated more with peers. This communication was both formal, within the professional-development sessions, and informal, in hallways between class periods and in the faculty room. A number of teachers reported that this mutual help around technology progressed into other domains (such as curriculum, creating lesson plans, instruction, and assessment).

Increased communication often translated into mutual cooperation. Teachers shared computers, helped out in a class that involved intensive technology use, or "loaned" their student technology helpers. Willingness to cooperate became part of the group culture. In these professional-development sessions, teachers were acknowledged and celebrated for their willingness to help and for their collegiality. Similarly, teachers were privately criticized if they were perceived as unwilling to assist colleagues.

That cooperation remained constant over time and matured into greater collaboration. Teachers, during the formal sharing sessions of the professional development, proposed working together on a certain activity. They expressed amazement at the commonalities across curricula and at the looping of content across grade levels. They began to plan activities together, and some began to teach together. Such collaboration marked a significant change in instruction, shifting it from an individual classroom activity to a collective enterprise. This process of co-creating activities and co-teaching allowed for students, classroom space, instruction, and curriculum to be viewed as shared entities and not just the province of one person. This collaboration also afforded a certain degree of professional intimacy, in that teachers allowed their colleagues to witness their strengths and weaknesses as communicators, classroom managers, instructors, curriculum designers—and as people.

During the second year, teachers' reliance on their professional-development provider also changed. Whereas in year one, teachers focused strongly on getting help from their facilitator, by year two, the facilitator was much less in demand. Teachers were turning to one another, and to their students, for help. They began to recognize that the locus of expertise was not outside the school. Plenty of expertise existed among Lafitte staff.

But most noticeable was teachers' evolving and changing relationship with students. Many, though not all, teachers appeared willing to view students as technology experts and frequently solicited student help with technology issues. A number of teachers reported that they regularly consulted students for technology advice. This increase in communication among teachers and students resulted in greater teacher–student cooperation, in terms of modifications of behavior toward one another. Greater collaboration was another result, seen in areas such as students designing criteria on which a project would be graded. And communication also helped create community, as students became teachers and teachers became learners in the area of technology.

FORMING A COMMUNITY OF PRACTICE

Paradoxically, the losses suffered at the beginning of the second year— of popular and supportive administrators, computer-knowledgeable colleagues, and a cadre of honors students—did not impede the greater community formation among teachers; rather, these challenges may have fostered community. First, many, if not most, of the teachers disagreed with the emphasis on traditional teaching, "back to basics," and test preparation. They all had worked hard to achieve some degree of instructional or technological change in their classrooms and had seen some measure of academic and behavior improvement as a consequence. On a personal level, most teachers enjoyed using cooperative and collaborative approaches. They felt—even when they complied with administrative mandates about "back to basics"—that a steady diet of traditional instruction was not in students' or teachers' best interests. Formerly fundamentalists themselves, they now scoffed with converts' zeal at the fundamentalism of test preparation: "That's not teaching. That's training."

Because teachers knew they would get little support from administrators, they formed a series of alliances to provide moral, intellectual, and logistical support. Many felt that they, and not the administrators, truly understood best classroom practices, and some of the greater connection resulted from this shared faith. However, because the bottom line was on attaining passing test scores, teachers had to make certain that a computer-based or learner-centered activity really could ensure the same success rate as a skills-based approach. Many teachers thus enlisted content-area peers and experienced practitioners, such as Louise, to help them with instruction. During the second year of the project, teachers met regularly, as well as informally, with content-area and other grade-level peers to plan activities and brainstorm ideas. Teachers who were able to form successful alliances or networks with peers were more likely to adhere to technology integration and learner-centered practices. Those who were not, or those who remained more isolated, tended to revert to more traditional approaches to instruction.

Second, following the loss of some of their more technically knowledgeable colleagues, teachers also came together to help one another in the area of technology. As one teacher remarked, "We used to wait for help, but now that they're gone, we get together and among the bunch of us, someone can figure out how to do what we want." Another reported, "We go around to each other and ask, 'What do you need?' and try to help. If we can't figure it out, we usually can find someone who can." This mutual assistance helped teachers feel more confident in their troubleshooting skills and served to acknowledge new "experts"—teachers who were previously unrecognized in terms of their technology skills. The mutual support system around technology allowed teachers to see the strength in working together and in forming networks and fostered a greater sense of mutual reliance and willingness to help among faculty. A *willingness* to help, not necessarily ability, seemed to be the quality most valued and appreciated.

Finally, with a smaller core of honors students and the subsequent elimination of many honors classes, even those teachers who had previously confined technology use and learner-centered approaches to their honors classes were forced to diffuse these same approaches to their "regular" students. Teachers reported that they were surprised not only by the quality of students' work—the professionalism of a word-processed report, the eye-catching quality of an electronic presentation—but also by students' academic ability. Students' work improved greatly when they were allowed to use technology, teachers said, and students were often more willing to tackle harder tasks.

The result was improved teacher–student relationships, even in special-education and low-achieving classes. For example, the special-education teacher had for a year and a half resisted allowing computers in her classes, predicting that her students would break them. When her students were given six discarded but functional Apple IIEs and a box of donated software, this teacher, who normally complained about her students, remarked incredulously, "I can't believe this! They're coming in during recess and lunch *begging* me to let them do their work! And it's excellent!" A history teacher was astonished when a student demonstrated his concept map of a particular event in Louisiana history using Inspiration software. "Wow. He's such a troublemaker. . . . I had no idea he knew so much."

During one professional-development session, a math teacher shared examples of students' work from a linear-equations project using the ingredients and unit prices of their favorite cereals. The teacher read a letter from one of her students, known to other teachers in attendance as a marginal student. Thanking the teacher for a project that was "real world" and that allowed for "creativity" and collaboration, the student mentioned that the combination of project-based math activities and computer use truly "prepared [us] for college and the working world" and was more effective than "the 12,000-year-old method" of textbook and questions.

THE ROLE OF VETERANS

The progression toward a community of practice could not have occurred at Lafitte without the school's cadre of veteran teachers. Oftentimes, the professional-development world holds an unstated view that instructional change and innovation will take hold in schools with the passing of the "old guard." Yet the experience at Lafitte Middle School contradicts this presumption.

For the most part, the veteran teachers were not innovators. They were non-ideological and pragmatic in their professional lives, not adherents of a particular educational "-ism." Veterans were results-oriented—aiming for outcomes such as better student behavior and increased academic performance. Any approach that could attain these two ends was embraced. Years of teaching experience had led them to become somewhat skeptical after weathering numerous educational fads, so they adopted a "this, too, shall pass" attitude toward many of the directives that came from the district. In light of their indifference toward so-called educational innovations, their enthusiastic embrace of technology and learner-centered teaching vested such approaches with a certain degree of credibility.

Further, many of the veteran teachers had been at Lafitte longer than their administrators and knew the students, families, instruction, and institutional culture better than the administrators did. Although she was not an administrator, Louise was the de facto leader of the school, and her opinion regarding instruction and computers carried more weight with colleagues than did that of the administrators.

Even though veteran teachers were "paper trained," they were well trained. Years of classroom experience meant familiarity with their content area, classroom management, instruction, and adolescent behavior. The benefits of experience gave them the confidence to try new instructional approaches, unlike their younger colleagues, many of whom still struggled to gain control of the classroom and to master their content area and pedagogy. Veterans focused on essentials: instruction, content, curriculum—not computers. Because of their "paper training," the computer would not supplant the curricular focus. It would serve as an instructional tool, when beneficial. When not useful, it would not be used.

Because many of the veteran teachers' computer skills remained modest, they did not get caught up in the "trees" of computers—operations or software tricks—but remained focused on the "forest": what computers could bring to learning, how they could help students do something more efficiently or in a better way, or how they could help students do something that would otherwise not be possible. These teachers' lack of proficiency with computers also meant that they allowed students to handle the technology, without interfering. And because veteran teachers commanded respect and were secure in their interactions with students, they were more likely than novice colleagues to allow or encourage students to teach them about computers.

Veterans also enjoyed the benefit of time spent with colleagues. Their years at Lafitte had resulted in the formation of strong personal and professional relationships, particularly among language arts teachers, many of whom had been at Lafitte for more than ten years. Participation in professional development provided a new dimension to these relationships and formalized many existing cooperative relationships, so that this seminal community expanded to include other language arts teachers, teachers from different subject areas, and those with less teaching experience. Veteran teachers such as Louise mentored and encouraged novice teachers, thus fostering a mutually supportive professional network. Her blunt admonitions and her generous help provided the necessary amounts of pressure and support to colleagues and made her an effective facilitator of change. Veterans' steadfast adherence to principles of good instruction and technology use in the face of administrative pressures served as both a model and moral to young teachers sometimes unsure of instructional decisions.

By becoming learners in the professional-development sessions, teachers began to empathize with their students as learners and in turn reflect on how they as teachers promoted or impeded learning. The conflict created by new administrators unsympathetic toward new instructional approaches and technology use further caused teachers to examine their newfound beliefs about learning. Those who did not buy into the new paradigm of instruction acceded to administrator demands that they focus more on "coverage"—lectures, drill, and test preparation. Those who believed in the new modes of instruction stood fast in the face of administrator demands and developed a supportive community with like-minded colleagues.

By learning from and with colleagues and students about technology and instructional practices, teachers became a community of learners. As the cognitive and affective pieces of learning translated into actual classroom application and behavioral changes, this community of learning matured into a community of *practice*. This is an important distinction, for the cognitive, intellectual, and affective changes that form part of learning do not always translate into behavioral changes. Mindful of students' academic successes in this new model of instruction, Lafitte teachers put their understanding of learning into practice in their classrooms, changing the way they taught; honing their newly developed skills through trial and error; learning from students; and advising, collaborating with, and encouraging colleagues in their shift toward a more meaningful and effective instructional approach.

NOTES

1. All names used in this book are pseudonyms.
2. This thought pattern was revealed in private conversations and e-mail exchanges between teachers and one of the authors.

5

Building a Vision: Toward an Intentional Community of Practice

When I decided to work here, I wanted to find out why minority children were not doing well on tests. Was it because they couldn't or because they were not being taught? Was it because they were not being given the quality education they deserved?

—Teacher, Starr Elementary School

A t Lafitte Middle School, a community of practice arose from grassroots origins and grew stronger in response to conflict. Teachers experienced cognitive dissonance about technology and new types of instruction. They also were faced with administrative edicts that they felt ignored and negated the best ways for students to learn. Although conflict was a powerful spur toward community formation, consensus can produce equally strong results.

Starr Elementary School, an urban neighborhood school serving a largely poor and minority population in a Texas city, followed this second path toward forming a community of practice. Starr was a new school, built by the district to reduce overcrowding in three other neighborhood schools.

The principal selected to lead Starr envisioned and designed the new school as a community for teachers, students, and their families. She and her school-based leadership team assembled a planning team consisting of themselves, an education professor from a local university, and two external consultants. Their task: establish a school that would employ the best practices in schooling in order to demonstrate that all children, regardless of race, ethnicity, or socioeconomic status, can be successful learners.

BUILDING A VISION: THE PLANNING PROCESS

The story of Starr's journey from an idea to a community of practice began with the principal and the planning process she initiated before the school opened its doors. With thirteen years of experience at an exemplary elementary school (so rated because of its state test scores), Carolyn was asked to become the principal of a new school set to open in the fall of the following academic year. Her former school was an early adopter of educational technology, and she was recognized by the district for her technology leadership.

Carolyn eagerly accepted her new challenge. She had grown up in the neighborhood to be served by the new school and felt that this assignment would give her an opportunity to demonstrate that success was possible for all learners. Whereas her former school was fairly homogeneous and affluent (90 percent of students were white, and only 13 percent were economically disadvantaged), Starr Elementary, with over 80 percent minority students and 83 percent economically disadvantaged, would serve a decidedly poorer and more diverse student clientele.

Starr provided Carolyn the opportunity to "get it right"—to consult educational specialists, to employ best practices in curriculum and instruction, to align the school's vision with student needs, to ensure that all teacher professional development matched this vision, and to create a community where teachers and students worked together to achieve excellence.

The planning team for Starr Elementary School met for three months to brainstorm, discuss best practices in education, share ideas and resources, and develop a plan for the new school. They discussed such topics as school organization, curriculum, instruction, assessment, community involvement, scheduling, teacher hiring, professional development, and community partnerships.

THE BUILDING

How could the building's physical structure, the curriculum, technology, and instructional practices be integrated to create the most effective communal environment for the children who would attend Starr Elementary? The planning team presented Carolyn with the latest research regarding technology integration, technology and instruction, and strategies for organizing schools to support "at-risk" learners. Books and journal articles were provided for the planning meetings, and the team read, discussed, and synthesized these ideas into concrete plans for the new school.

Family ties are extremely important in the culture of the children who attend Starr. Therefore, it was decided to organize children and teachers into "villages" to create a more familial environment that would support both the children and their parents; cultivate connections among teachers, parents, and the community (Martinez, Perez & Cook, 1998); and offer a support structure for teachers. Siblings in different grade levels would be placed in the same villages so that teachers, as a team, could share responsibility for children from the same families.

How could the architectural design of the school support community building? The gym, cafeteria, library, and reception area were placed in adjacent spaces in the center block of the building. Four separate wings or "halls" radiated from two sides of the center, connected by short perpendicular hallways, similar to an H with a thick crosspiece. This arrangement allowed for possible future expansion. Most important, by organizing classes across the grade levels into each hall, four smaller and nested subcommunities or "schools within a school" could be created.

Both the layout and the organization would serve to enhance community. Teachers would work together in horizontal teams across similar grades and vertical teams from pre-kindergarten to fifth grade. The vertical teams would be located in the same physical space (the hall) and would coordinate a student's educational program from preschool through the fifth grade. A student would stay with this vertical team of teachers, one teacher for each grade level from pre-kindergarten through fifth grade, and would go through classes with the same group of students for as long as he or she attended the school. ("Looping," the practice of keeping students with the same teacher for several years during elementary school, was also discussed. However, concerns were raised about what might happen if a student and teacher were not right for each other but were paired for several years, so this idea was eventually abandoned.) Because the school would serve a large number of English language learners, one hall in the school was designated the bilingual hall, in which classes would be taught in both Spanish and English. Vertical teams of teachers would meet regularly to discuss student progress, thus creating an organizational support for the development of a community of practice within each hall.

TECHNOLOGY AND INSTRUCTIONAL PHILOSOPHY

Carolyn was clear that her new school must have technology integrated in every subject and in every classroom. Although her former school had been one of the most technology-rich in the district, Carolyn voiced disappointment with the ways teachers there had employed technology in their classrooms. Their use of computers did not, in her view, truly capitalize on technology's full instructional potential.

Hand in hand with technology, then, came the issue of establishing a school-wide instructional philosophy, one that would support both technology and community. The planning team examined and discussed problem-based and project-based learning, research on cognition and how it could inform classroom practices, and the role of technology in this type of environment. The team determined that learner-centered instruction supported by technology would match Starr's goals. To help create this type of environment, Starr teachers would participate in two years (seventy-two hours) of technology professional development.

TEACHER HIRING

Teachers, of course, were the critical element in realizing Starr's vision. Demands on this new faculty would be high. Teachers would need to agree to work in teams, collaborate with peers, commit to a learner-centered instructional approach, use technology in ways that demonstrably improved student learning, and devote long hours to attaining the twin goals of community and excellence. The planning team developed an interview design that included standardized inventories, interview questions, and responses to written prompts. This process would help Carolyn determine which teachers were best qualified to support the new school's vision.

Teachers were required to arrive one hour before the interview to complete the three inventories[1] and respond to the following statement in writing and/or through drawings: "Describe the learning environment in which you would most like to teach." More than twenty potential questions were designed for the principal to ask the teachers during the interview.

After Carolyn began the interview process, she shared the results with the planning team in an e-mail message:

> I have been very pleased with how excited and enthusiastic almost all of them have been about coming to a new school. They really liked the vision for the new school. Many of them said they wished they could teach with tables and chairs instead of desks before I ever said anything about that. Three of the teachers gave me drawings of how they would like to set up their classrooms with tables and chairs and centers, so I am very encouraged with what I am seeing so far. Unfortunately, most of the teachers I have interviewed have pretty limited experience with technology because they just had little or nothing in their schools, but they were very enthusiastic about learning. All of their enthusiasm has made me even more excited about this new school.

Participation in professional development would address these technology weaknesses. Once they were selected, Carolyn welcomed the faculty in a letter. "I am so pleased and excited that Starr Elementary School will be opening its doors for the first time with the most competent, committed, and enthusiastic professionals in the city," she wrote. "Each one of you has so many strengths and so much talent and expertise to share. I feel honored to have the opportunity to work with you to begin a tradition of excellence and success for Starr Elementary School's students."

A COMMUNITY OF PRACTICE IN PRACTICE

Starr Elementary School opened its doors to 509 pre-kindergarten to fifth-grade children. Many of the foundations had been laid for a school that would promote both excellence and community, physically (in terms of the architectural design and layout of the school), organizationally (through horizontal and vertical teaming of teachers), instructionally (with a learner-centered, technology-integrated, theme-based instructional approach), in terms of leadership, and in terms of resources (all teachers would participate in technology professional development). Would these approaches promote excellence and foster a sense of community, as intended? What other elements would need to be in place to enable these outcomes?

PHYSICAL INFRASTRUCTURE

One of the first orders of business was to name each of the hallways. A school-wide contest determined that the halls would be named after space vehicles, such as Challenger and Voyager. Each hall accommodated approximately 125 pre-kindergarten through fifth-grade students and their vertical team of teachers. These vertical teams included students of a wide range of abilities and ages who worked in groups based on their needs, strengths, interests, and learning styles, not solely on their grade level.

ORGANIZATION: TEAMING

The vertical teams of pre-kindergarten to fifth-grade teachers from each hall met biweekly to plan a monthly cross-grade thematic unit. For the first time in many of their careers, teachers were able to work together with colleagues in other grades, collaborating on cross-grade activities that helped their own practice. Teachers commented that they loved meeting in their vertical teams. They were learning in ways they had never experienced before. But the greatest benefits of the vertical teaming, according to teachers, accrued to students. One teacher said that the teaming "works really well because we have the families, the complete family from kindergarten through fifth grade, in our hall and the children stay together as long as they are at this school. They get to work with their brothers and sisters from the upper grades and the lower grades. They come visit us and they show us their projects, what they're learning in class, and that gives them a warmer feeling at school, because they know their brothers and sisters are close by."

Another teacher described the benefits of vertical teaming in this way: "I've explained to my children that Ms. D is going to be their teacher next year. So when they go over there and show her what they are doing in my class, they are really proud. She gets very impressed with them and tells them, 'Wow. You're already doing that. My class is doing that, too.' They're not going to be so afraid to go in there, because they have already done some of that work in my class, and it will be a smooth transition."

In addition to their vertical cross-grade teams, teachers worked together with their grade-level colleagues in horizontal teams. Grade-level team meetings were held once each month to bring teachers together. This teaming created a structure in which teachers had dedicated time to discuss issues about teaching and learning on that grade level. In addition, multiple committees were established to focus on practical issues. Teachers chaired these committees, thus distributing leadership across the campus.

INSTRUCTION: TECHNOLOGY INTEGRATION

One of Carolyn's goals was to see technology used so that it truly promoted student learning, allowing students to learn in ways that otherwise would not have been possible. The school was intentionally designed without a computer lab, to support the integration of technology into the daily instruction of each teacher. At least one multimedia computer with direct Internet access was installed in every classroom. Seven classrooms had four Internet-connected multimedia computers, and in the library five computers were available for class use. In addition to computers, teachers had telephones in their classrooms and access to voice mail. Thus technology supported ongoing communication among teachers, administrators, and the community through e-mail and telephone.

The presence of technology in each classroom and the emphasis on intra-grade and inter-grade collaboration resulted in numerous theme-based, school-wide technology-integrated collaborations. For example, one fourth-grade social studies teacher organized a school-wide election for governor. Students researched the two-party system, created profiles of the candidates including their stances on some of the issues, and researched the basics of election law. Fourth graders registered all students in the school using a voter registration database they and their teachers had created. When students voted, their names were checked off the voter rolls by students and the ballot was placed in a secure container. After the voting had ended, the fourth graders entered the votes along with some demographic data that was also collected on the ballot. This way, the results could be queried and posted by grade level, gender, and other variables. The election was a great success, with 372 of Starr's 509 students voting.

In another example of such collaboration, a first-grade teacher enlisted the entire school in the development of a school song, which was illustrated by her students using drawing software and posted to the school's Web site. And in a cross-grade reading project, fifth-grade and first-grade students were paired to read books selected by the first graders. This project was designed to improve the reading skills of both the older and younger students. One outcome of this project was the development of an alphabet book, made for the kindergarten students by the reading pairs using multimedia-development software.

LEADERSHIP

Carolyn, her assistant principal, a projects coordinator, and the school counselor formed the school's leadership team. The projects coordinator led the planning, development, and implementation of curricular thematic units, wrote grants, and worked with teachers to develop learner-centered, technology-rich learning environments. All members of the leadership team participated in the technology professional development provided for teachers.

Carolyn had high expectations for faculty, including flexibility, positive attitudes, home–school involvement, and teamwork. In return, she rewarded teachers verbally and provided enjoyable settings in which to learn together, such as a faculty get-togethers and team building at a retreat site outside town.

ONGOING PROFESSIONAL DEVELOPMENT

When teachers were hired to work in the new school, they knew they were committed to participate in technology professional development.

All teachers signed a letter of commitment, and the principal gave them a form, titled "Expectations of the Successful Starr Elementary School Staff Member," that described the necessity of participating in the professional development. The entire faculty and the leadership team attended this professional development together over the course of two years.

The professional development solidified the formation of a community among Starr's teachers in several ways. First, Carolyn, professional-development facilitators, and other members of the planning team had engineered the conditions within which a community of practice could take root.

Community cannot, however, be mandated or designated by fiat. People need to come together around issues of common interest. Further, they must want to come together and work together. The professional-development sessions provided a context within which the entire faculty, all of whom were new to Starr and few of whom had previously known one another, could meet on a regular basis.

The professional development also furnished issues (instruction, technology, improved student learning) around which faculty could work together. Teachers certainly met in their horizontal and vertical teams apart from the professional development, but the professional-development sessions strengthened this teaming arrangement by having teachers work with their teammates and with people from outside their team.

Because teachers could meet and work with their colleagues from other halls, the professional development also helped them to feel part of a larger school-wide community. One teacher described the benefits of school-wide thematic material in this way:

> We are working on thematic units school-wide. The first was the community, building our community, and it was done school-wide. The next thematic unit is oceans. We are excited about that because some of the teachers went on a research trip to learn more about the ocean and the things that we can teach our children. They brought back a lot of specimens to show the children samples of things that are in the ocean, and that will help us to bring the ocean to them since we can't go all the way over there on a field trip.

In addition to encouraging community, professional-development sessions helped Starr's faculty develop a shared vision and understanding of instruction that linked to actual classroom practice. One of the initial activities required teachers to work together in small groups to create visual representations of how children learn, without using words or numbers. Using these visual depictions, the small groups explained their ideas to one another and then connected these ideas to learning theory in a reflective discussion. One of the teachers described the impact of this activity as follows: "After we did that activity in the training, I had the feeling that we're all working together, and we all have the same ideas, feelings, and philosophies about where we want our children to be when they leave the elementary program and move into the middle school."

In another professional-development activity, teachers circulated through stations set up as learning centers. One station was a digital camera center, another was a computer center, a third was a print materials center, and a fourth instructed teachers to collect their ideas about "our community" in anticipation of creating an exhibit to showcase their community and its unique features. In conjunction with this professional-development activity, Carolyn organized a bus tour so teachers could visit the neighborhoods served by the school and use digital cameras to take pictures of the homes, churches, businesses, parks, and other sights along the route. The digital images were used to create electronic presentations about "our community," which became the basis for the first school-wide thematic unit the teachers planned when the school year began. During the reflection following the community activity, Carolyn joined with the teachers to discuss what they had seen on the bus tour and what that meant for them and their teaching practice for the coming year.

The professional development helped teachers improve instruction. Once the school year began, teaching was observed in every classroom. Unlike teachers at Lafitte Middle School, teachers at Starr were using a wide variety of teaching practices at the start of the school year. It was expected that learner-centered practices would be employed in all classrooms, as Carolyn had selected teachers whose philosophy and approach were aligned with the goals established for the school. However, not all teachers successfully employed learner-centered approaches. Although many teachers employed hands-on activities, learner-centered approaches, and discussion strategies such as eliciting prior knowledge, accepting a variety of responses, and encouraging students to further explain their responses to questions, others were far more traditional—leading the whole class through a lesson with all the children working on the same activities at the same time.

The professional-development sessions helped teachers better understand learner-centered instruction by immersing them in activities that were interdisciplinary, inquiry based, and highly active, and that modeled a learner-centered instructor. Over time, observations revealed classrooms that were increasingly learner-centered in design. The students were at the center of the activity, with the teacher in the role of facilitator or working with small groups of students. These classrooms were organized so that students worked individually or in small groups at learning centers, or on small-group hands-on activities, while the teacher served as facilitator or

coach. Learning centers, in which students at each table worked on a separate activity that constituted part of a larger unit, seemed to be most popular among Starr's teachers. As one teacher explained:

> Most of the school is working with centers in the classroom, because we feel
> that if the children take ownership in their learning, they are learning at their
> own pace and in their own style and through whatever they want to do at the
> center. When they get tired of working in one center, they go to another cen-
> ter. They're making their own choices, and I think that helps them become
> lifelong learners. They are actively participating in the centers, and that helps
> them be successful.

Technology professional development also helped teachers get accus-
tomed to the physical accommodations that are part of a learner-centered
approach. Despite their philosophical agreement with the goals at Starr,
the teachers needed to make many adjustments. For example, all classrooms were furnished with round tables and chairs in sizes appropriate to
the ages of the children, as the planning team believed this furniture
would support small-group work and cooperative learning. There were
no desks to be put in rows, so teachers familiar with that sort of classroom
arrangement had to learn to deal with small groups of students clustered
about tables, as this comment illustrates:

> I had to try different ideas to see what worked for me. . . . The round tables,
> the cubbies, the centers, working with an individual, with small groups,
> while other groups were busy. That was new for me. I'd never worked like
> that before. . . . I was constantly going into everybody's room and asking,
> "How are you doing this? How are you doing that?" And everybody had dif-
> ferent ideas.

By working together in activities in which they themselves used tables instead of desks, by participating in a forum in which the whole faculty
could share and discuss ideas and solutions to certain challenges, and by
developing feelings of trust and collegiality as a result of frequent formal
interaction, teachers could help one another devise strategies and develop
attitudes that could assist them in adjusting to the many components of a
learner-centered environment.

Starr's teachers became more comfortable with technology through
professional development. They began with a wide range of technology
skills, most having some general computer skills and familiarity with
word-processing and e-mail, but little experience in integrating various
technology applications into actual classroom instruction. And, like their
colleagues at Lafitte, teachers came together to help one another learn
how to use computers, integrate them into classroom activities, and plan

instructional activities in such a way that tentative computer-using teachers would feel supported.

Working together to create lessons that employed computers gave the experienced teachers new lenses through which to view their former ways of teaching. "It left me fired up to present old ideas in a new way. I kept saying, 'I never thought of teaching that with the computer.'"

Teachers noted that the professional development increased their confidence in using technology in the classroom. For some, it "opened [their] eyes and mind to ways of using technology," as one teacher commented. The sessions in which teachers presented to the other teachers lessons they had developed were especially valuable. As one teacher put it, "The most useful thing to me was seeing how the staff grew in confidence in incorporating technology. The 'Show and Tell' sessions were great. I saw a great deal of enthusiasm from fellow teachers and an eagerness to implement ideas that were shared."

Finally, meeting together in professional-development sessions that were aligned with the school's goals created a real forum for sharing ideas and working together to translate ideas into actual classroom practice. Being in the midst of new ways of doing what had long been routine provided an impetus for teachers to share ideas and talk to one another, looking for solutions that worked in this new kind of environment. One teacher reported that this was the most valuable thing about the professional development for her—"breaking into groups and talking and sharing with teachers closer to our grade levels to get new ideas and know you have support in the school." These were the very conversations Carolyn had hoped would occur.

USING TECHNOLOGY TO SUPPORT
THE COMMUNITY OF PRACTICE

Collecting and Analyzing Data

In addition to the careful planning, the creation of a vision, selection of teachers who shared this vision, and choosing professional development aligned with the school's vision, Carolyn set in place other supports that fostered academic excellence and further solidified a community of practice at the school level.

Like every school, Starr faced the often-conflicting demands of state testing pressures and belief in the preeminence of learner-centered approaches to student achievement. Carolyn wanted teachers to reflect on student achievement data, and she encouraged instructional planning based on data analysis. How could she put this information into teachers' hands in a way that would allow them to analyze which students were learning, and which were not? What would help teachers plan more efficiently and effectively?

Carolyn understood the value of using technology to store and analyze data, since she was familiar with the work that was being done on her campus by the school's technology director and special projects coordinator. Before the school opened, they had created a database that housed the student information collected each year on student record cards (students' addresses, phone numbers, parent names, emergency contact information, grade level, immunization records, and so on). Carolyn and the leadership team had used this information when scheduling students into classes, to ensure that siblings were assigned to classrooms in the same halls.

However, Carolyn wanted more information that could update her, the teachers, and parents about student progress. Carolyn and her leadership team examined existing additional academic data and considered how it might be linked to the student informational database and set up on a central server so teachers could enter information and access the data from their classroom computers. The technology coordinator set about creating such a system.

Carolyn also decided that she and the teachers could not wait until the state administered its annual test in the spring to assess whether students were mastering the curriculum. She found that the state education agency's Web site contained prior years' versions of the test. She and the teachers discussed how they might use those tests periodically during the school year to benchmark student progress and target instruction more effectively to improve student learning.

Once teachers had administered these sample tests, the database was adapted so that teachers could enter the results and generate progress reports for each student in their class. Carolyn also examined the progress reports to help her determine which classrooms were experiencing success, and in what areas. With data in hand, Carolyn met with teachers in faculty meetings and made the results of the benchmark tests public. She pointed out how students in some classrooms were more successful than others. Since students had been assigned heterogeneously to classrooms, teachers could not suggest that some classes were inherently less capable than others.

Peer Coaching

Carolyn set in motion several strategies to assist teachers whose students were struggling with benchmarks. First, teachers whose students were struggling received additional assistance and resources. One form of such assistance was to pair a teacher from a more successful classroom with one whose students were experiencing less success, to work together to target students' instructional needs.

Next, Carolyn worked with teachers in individual goal-setting meetings to examine student data in that teacher's class. Carolyn and the teacher set achievement goals for the students and learning goals for the teacher, thus identifying areas in which the teacher wanted and needed help.

Third, to support data analysis and targeted instruction, Starr teachers were provided with opportunities to meet and discuss instructional strategies that worked for their students. One teacher who was particularly successful with teaching children to read became a mentor teacher for others who were struggling. She would visit classrooms and observe the teacher, then teach demonstration lessons while the teacher observed her. Next, the two teachers would meet to discuss what seemed to be working with students. One experienced teacher explained why this peer-mentoring program was important to the school:

> New teachers don't have a bag of tricks or strategies. Eventually their bag will get full. It is tiny now, but mine is large, so I can share my ideas. It's really fun to do that. I'm a coach, an advocate for all teachers. I'm not an evaluator. I can't be judgmental. We have a mentor program—we meet monthly. Each teacher is paired with an experienced teacher who is also a learner, not judgmental, having people skills, and they go in and teach lessons for the novice teachers—model lessons.

These examples of working together around student needs—paired peer assistance, working together with the principal, and formal meeting opportunities for teachers—supplemented other mechanisms for community building, such as vertical and horizontal teaming and school-wide professional development. Teachers and administrators came together around a common issue (student achievement on benchmarks) and worked collaboratively on content, curriculum, instruction, and technology use to help students become more successful.

Planning Instruction

To help teachers develop instructional plans for when and how they would teach particular objectives in the curriculum across the school year, Carolyn returned to the technology director and the special projects director for a technology solution. They created a new database to house the state's curriculum for reading and mathematics. Now teachers at every grade level could access the objectives and student expectations for these two subject areas via their classroom computer. The database was further designed to allow teachers to develop instructional plans that were linked to both the curriculum objectives and the scores on student benchmark tests. The technology professional development supported these efforts. One of the professional-development sessions focused on developing and using databases and helped teachers learn to use their school's database system. Another session provided work time for teacher teams to develop activities that would address shared student academic needs as revealed in benchmark testing and to enter these plans into the school's database.

Teachers continued, during horizontal team meetings, to collaboratively develop weekly grade-level instructional plans targeting the curriculum objectives that would be the focus for that week. These objectives were not everything the teachers taught, but they were objectives that every teacher on that grade level would be teaching as part of the week's instruction. Housing them in the school's centralized database made them available to all of Starr's teachers. Collaboratively, teachers also developed a set of standard interventions that they could use with students who were struggling, and these were added to the interface so that teachers could select interventions from a range of choices. Based on the students' performance and the objectives, teachers might decide that students needed extra tutoring or that a new learning center addressing a particular objective was needed. The database for instructional plans allowed teachers to indicate which interventions were to be applied for students who had not yet mastered these objectives.

Starr's use of technology supported an ongoing process for aligning the school's vision with the nuts and bolts of curriculum, standards, instruction, and assessment, as well as the professional development needed to support this process. Starr developed a coherent system for teaching and learning: Teachers could follow their students' progress on the benchmark assessments and isolate which objectives were or were not mastered by individual students in their classes. They could then focus on interventions for objectives the students had not mastered and spend less time on objectives on which students performed well. The professional development could help them devise instructional strategies and activities to support these interventions.

Database technology also provided Carolyn with information she could use in meetings with teachers, both individually and as an entire faculty. She could follow up with them about how and when they went about teaching the curriculum and the results they were getting with the children. And she could provide the support teachers needed to improve their instructional practice by targeting additional resources, such as a peer mentor, a content specialist, or professional development. There would be no excuses if students were not mastering the content. But there would be lots of support and guidance.

Despite this apparent focus on testing, teachers reported that this technology solution freed them from focusing on the test and allowed them more time to teach the curriculum. They did not have to spend time working on objectives that students had already mastered. They could move on with some assurance that the students would do well when the time came for them to take the statewide standardized assessment. One teacher explained this phenomenon in this way:

> We are not a test-driven school. When people hear about all the things we are doing with data and all the benchmark testing we are doing, they think we are focused on the state test. We are not. The reason we are doing this is so we don't have to teach to the test. The idea is to use the data, see where the needs are, focus in on those needs, and then focus in on the other content you want to teach. Don't drop science, social studies, and the other crucial subjects. Just make sure you are covering the bases for the test. This database helps the teachers focus in on those needs rather than floundering around trying to figure out what they need to be teaching.

And Starr's approach worked—the students did very well. Using state-standardized assessment data from students' previous schools, Carolyn was able to calculate how Starr would have been rated using those scores. According to students' past scores on the state achievement test, Starr would have been categorized as a low-performing school. Carolyn wanted Starr to be rated exemplary, just as her former school in an affluent section of town had been. To meet this standard, over 90 percent of the students had to pass all sections of the state-standardized assessment, and passing rates had to be the same for all subgroups of students. Although Starr did not meet this goal the first year, it was rated as a recognized school. Only one area fell below the level needed for an exemplary rating.

Starr's test results raised issues among the faculty concerning minority achievement. One African American teacher challenged the others to think hard about their expectations for students: "In a faculty meeting the other day one of the teachers kept saying, 'The African American children—that's why we aren't an exemplary school.' And I said, 'Okay, why? They are no different from anyone else. You have no evidence that they cannot learn as well as any other children. Why are they scoring low?'"

This teacher explained later how her understanding of her students had changed since Starr opened its doors:

> When I decided to work here, I had one question I needed answered. I wanted to find out why minority children were not doing well on tests. Was it because they couldn't, or because they were not being taught? Was it because they were not being given the quality education they deserved? I know the answer to that question now. Before I came here, I was looking through

rose-colored glasses—kids are wonderful and all well-behaved. When I came here I was like everyone else because I had been blinded all those years. I was not living in the real world—at least that part of the world that the kids see. Now I look at them one at a time. You have to be a tough, loving teacher, but when you look at them one by one, you will know that every child deserves the best and we need to rid ourselves of racism and classism. We have to take children as they come to us. It's not easy to have this vision and smile through it all. You have to fight.

Starr attained exemplary status in only two years. To celebrate this success, a community-wide celebration was planned to showcase the students' and teachers' hard work. Carolyn believed that celebrations were an important part of building a community of practice. Parents and district leaders, including the superintendent of schools, as well as community partners, were invited to the celebration. Awards were given to teachers and students for outstanding performance in a wide range of areas. In the school auditorium, students, teachers, parents, and community members joined together to chant, "Starr is exemplary! Starr is exemplary! Starr is exemplary!"

Carolyn encouraged the teachers publicly for all the work they had already done toward promoting Starr's vision of both academic excellence and creating a collaborative community:

> We've come together and started to bond. We still have a ways to go. I'm really proud of you. In these goal-setting conferences we are having, I'm getting to know each of you better. Some of you have told me that you don't know me very well. It will take time to build that trust factor. But we are on the right track. Although I know we all get frustrated because there is so much more we want to do and get done, we have to look back on how much we've already done. Just a few months ago we didn't even know each other at all. We didn't even know one another's names. And look how we know each other now and talk with one another and fight with each other! We've really come a long way.

CONCLUSION

The creation of a community of practice at Starr Elementary was an intentional and planned process. School leaders intended to create a campus that facilitated community in the following ways:

- Through the *physical* infrastructure and layout of the school: centralized common areas, self-contained halls, no computer labs, tables and chairs rather than desks in classrooms to allow greater ease of students working together

- Through *instructional* elements: learner-centered pedagogy supported by technology, collaborative learning, the integration of technology in every classroom and every content area, thematic units, and a learning centers approach
- Through *collaborative* elements: vertical and horizontal teacher teaming and school-wide ongoing professional development to help teachers come together to implement the school's goal of academic excellence for students

Community was also facilitated by technology use. Teachers came together to help one another learn how to use technology. They also used technology-based thematic activities to connect with other classrooms and other grades. Equally, though, technology, in the form of the school's centralized database that analyzed student outcomes and allowed teachers to target instructional activities to particular outcomes, was instrumental in the formation of a community of practice. The database allowed for the organization and retrieval of discrete information that allowed teachers to see where students needed help and where they as teachers needed assistance in helping students. Because of the information revealed by this technology, teachers came together with colleagues, individual peers, and the principal to deliberately reflect on instructional decisions, refine instructional practice, receive and give support and assistance, and work together around a common goal—improved student performance.

Starr serves as an example of a holistic approach toward creating a community of practice. The school was built with a distinct vision in mind. Its physical and instructional organization supported this vision. Professional development was aligned with the school's vision and helped expand teachers' smaller communities of practice in their halls to a school-wide community and even into the community at large. The school is an all-too-infrequent example of coherence, with its vision, curriculum, instructional philosophy, technology, and outcomes aligned and articulated to achieve a common goal: the success of every child in the school.

NOTE

1. Three standard inventory assessments were used: "A Teacher Attitude Inventory," by J. R. Whitmore (1974); "Scales for the Measurement of Innovativeness," by H. T. Hunt, K. Joseph, and C. D. Cook (1977); and "Computer Technologies and Teacher Education: The Measurement of Attitudes and Self-Efficacy," by M. B. Kinzie and A. B. Delcourt (1991).

6

No Matter What: Leadership and Communities of Practice

I'll do anything that's legal to provide the children with what they need—to have the skills and knowledge they need. I won't break the law, but I'll do anything I can to provide that. And technology is a critical piece.

—Enrique Gonzalez

The development of a community of practice at Benito Juarez Elementary was an evolutionary process that emerged from the ideals and vision of a strong principal, Enrique Gonzalez. He was passionate about providing whatever the children in his school needed, and he inspired his faculty to adopt the same attitude. With the help of a lead teacher for technology who had a passion of her own for learner-centered practice, the support of the district in which the school resides, and teachers who voluntarily took on the extra work required to transform their practice with technology, Juarez Elementary embarked on its journey toward a community of practice.

ABOUT THE SCHOOL

Juarez Elementary served its children, grades one through five, along the banks of the Rio Grande, in an area known as the Upper Valley. Ninety-four percent of the students were Hispanic, and 5 percent were white. All of the students were economically disadvantaged, and 53 percent were classified as English language learners. Connections to Mexico, where most families originated, were strong. Although it was located near an interstate highway, the small, primarily agricultural community Juarez served was isolated from surrounding communities and suffered from a lack of paved roads and adequate housing. Community leaders hoped that the interstate highway would be widened and that access roads to the town would be built, which would make the area more attractive to developers.

Juarez Elementary had forty-three teachers, three professional support personnel, two campus administrators, and twelve educational aides. Eight teachers were male. The faculty was fairly evenly split between white and Hispanic teachers. Most of the teachers had more than five years of teaching experience.

Juarez Elementary was part of a large nearby school district for forty-eight years. In 1959 the people of the town voted to incorporate as an independent school district. More schools were constructed as the town's student population increased. The Juarez Elementary building also expanded from the original one-room school in the district to include more classrooms and a gymnasium. Recently, a new building was constructed to house first through third grades and special education, with four multimedia computers and a printer in each of the eighteen new classrooms. In addition, the new building housed the administrative offices, the cafeteria, and the library, which contained twelve multimedia computers.

The district had an early commitment to technology integration, targeting its resources first on designated technology "innovators" and creating the position of "lead teacher for technology." This lead teacher worked with other teachers throughout the district to help them integrate technology in their classrooms. By providing teachers with one-on-one assistance and conducting demonstration lessons for teaching with technology, she reinforced the district's professional development and helped set expectations for technology use. Computers were placed in individual classrooms connected by a network system with open architecture. Software was purchased for core subject areas by grade level.

VISIONS FOR THE FUTURE

Juarez Elementary benefited from strong district leadership that held a clear vision for the school's future. The school's principal, Enrique Gonzalez, was a vital force in creating, maintaining, and realizing this vision.

Gonzalez grew up in the area. He went to work at an early age and did not receive his university degree until he was well into adulthood. He referred to the students as *"mi hijo"* and *"mi hija,"* terms of endearment that translate as "my son" and "my daughter." He was committed to the community and proactive and forward-thinking regarding technology and school reform. It was his idea to house the lower grades in the new building and to implement technology in those classes. He reasoned that he could more easily convince the community to invest in technology for the upper elementary grades at a later date. By placing the younger children in the technology-rich classrooms, he could ensure they also had access to these resources.

"One of the areas that was a dream of mine when I came here," he said, "was to push technology. I feel like I'm always selling—I'm always selling ideas and projects. I'm always selling people on moving forward and developing certain skills. This area is one of the poorest in the country. The school is 100 percent free and reduced lunch. Technology is an important sell in this community because unless we provide access to technology and training and support here in the building, it doesn't happen."

Gonzalez envisioned that all the children in his school would use technology to build skills he believed were essential to their success in the world. His unwavering belief in the power of technology to change the lives of the low-income children who attended Juarez Elementary was the basis for the community of practice at the school.

Another academic focus of the school was bilingual education. The goal was that all children would be fully fluent in Spanish and English by the time they left the school in fifth grade. Classrooms were organized in three primary ways to accomplish this goal: monolingual classrooms, where the only language taught was English; bilingual classrooms, where the teachers and the students learned, spoke, read, and wrote in both Spanish and English; and dual-language classrooms, where a Spanish language teacher and an English language teacher worked together with two groups of students to provide both Spanish and English instruction. Any parent could request that their children be placed in any of these programs.

USING TECHNOLOGY

In addition to his overarching vision for the students' future, Enrique Gonzalez had a vision for the way in which technology would be used in classrooms at the school. He knew that transforming the school would be a long and gradual process and that teachers would need support along the way:

> You are talking about a major paradigm shift, . . . from one way [of teaching] to another, if you are going to incorporate the technology the way we want it done. To get this kind of change, of course, you need gentle, constant pressure

with somebody pushing, and at the same time showing you what to do over a long span of time. We're not talking about six months or a year. We're talking about a three- to five-year process.

He also believed that it would not work to try to force teachers to change.

We told them that it was going to be a supportive process. It wasn't going to be, "You have to do it." It was going to be, "We need for you to start working with us. You have this entire year of constant support, no requirement for documentation unless sometimes we just want to see what you are doing. We want you to try. We want you to play, to experiment with it." We really worked very hard to create a non-threatening environment for them to begin to do this.

Gonzalez made staffing changes to accommodate teachers who were not interested in professional development. One teacher transferred to another school in the district, and two teachers moved to different grade levels, to avoid participating. All teachers of grades one through three were to participate, as each of their classrooms had just been given four computers and a printer.

Several supports were put in place to assist Juarez's teachers in attaining Enrique's vision. First, he asked the upper-grade teachers to work with the computer lab manager to integrate technology into their lessons and to stay with their students during computer class. This cooperative approach contrasted with the regular practice of teachers dropping off students at the computer lab to complete a separate computer lesson with the computer lab teacher. Next, Enrique arranged for student mentors from the high school to work with younger students in the elementary school lab. Finally, Enrique arranged for the district's lead teacher, Ms. Arbusto, to provide technology support to the teachers of grades one to three.

Ms. Arbusto attended all the professional-development sessions and provided makeup sessions for those teachers who could not attend on scheduled days. Her presence in the district and on the campus provided an ongoing support system for teachers. She explained that this professional development fit with what she had done as a classroom teacher:

I was teaching at a Catholic high school and the sisters were upset with the noise that was coming out of my room. I did not lecture. My students were working in groups. They were creating their own projects, but once I met the technology, I immediately saw what it could do for the way I had been teaching for many, many years. It's really exciting to me to see now that there is a name for what I have been doing, for what I know works.

Just as at Lafitte and Starr, facilitators met with teachers and collected information on their concerns about using technology and learner-centered practices. Teachers had many specific questions and worries: "Will technology be a substitute for learning?" "I only have one computer available." "I won't be making my classroom presentations on the computer." "Each student will have different needs. How can I coordinate that? How will I manage the classroom?" "What's the best way to control Internet access?" "How do you start letting students have more control?"

These and other concerns about the chaos that might erupt when students worked at centers or in cooperative groups were utmost on many teachers' minds. Enrique assured them that they should just try and that he would support them. One teacher described having felt she had failed miserably at her first attempt at cooperative learning. She went to Enrique in tears. He consoled her, saying, "Don't worry. Just wait a while and try it again." She talked with other teachers, got some pointers, and made another attempt. This time she felt the activity was a success. "I never would have tried it again if Mr. Gonzalez had not encouraged me to try again and if the other teachers weren't so willing to help me."

The technology professional development also provided encouragement to teachers who, like Ms. Arbusto, were already using learner-centered approaches but needed to add technology to their classroom practices. About midway through the first year of the professional-development sessions, Antonio, a third-grade teacher, invited teachers to his classroom so he could share a cross-classroom project in which his and four other classrooms were studying the Aztec, Olmec, and Mayan cultures of Mesoamerica. Authentic activities focusing on the food, music, mathematics, scientific discoveries, and literature of these cultures formed part of the project. Antonio admitted that he had not used computers in the past but had at last overcome his reluctance. "I am terrible with computers. I was worried about it. And I was projecting my inadequacies on my students."

During his impromptu classroom demonstration, he showed the other teachers his students' work. He invited the other teachers to participate in the Mesoamerica project, as well. He explained that he chose a daily helper to assist other students in using the computer center. Although he still found it embarrassing when the children knew more than he did, one strategy he said had helped him was to "just act like you forgot." By the following school year, Antonio had successfully applied for a grant enabling the teachers to create a Web site to share information with colleagues about their Mesoamerica project.

Over the course of the two years of professional development, teachers opened up their practice and invited others to collaborate with them on a variety of teaching and learning activities. The second-grade team, in particular, established close ties. One second-grade teacher described this working relationship in this way: "I've had really good response with the other teachers at my grade level. They actually plan with me so much that basically, second grade does everything together. It's very nice to have that unity. We have a really good group."

Another teacher described how she depended on one of her colleagues for help with technology. "The training has helped me to understand how to ask for help. Because I'm not as computer literate as Adriana, whenever I have a problem, I go straight to her. 'Adriana, I did something wrong here. Help me.'"

Like teachers at Starr and Lafitte, teachers at Juarez Elementary claimed that the most valuable results of the professional development were learning to use technology and sharing ideas with so many other teachers on their campuses. Comments confirmed the usefulness of a technology-instruction approach that emphasized comfort over proficiency and that focused on technology as one piece in the classroom system: "I appreciated that you showed me just the right amount of technology for me to understand it better. You didn't show me all of the details and make it confusing." "You helped me see that when something goes wrong with my computer, it's not always my fault. Sometimes the computer has problems, and I don't need to know why it didn't work, or to blame myself." "This opened my mind up to a new world of possibilities and different ways to use the computer." "I am more relaxed about using the computer now. I still have a long way to go, but it feels good not to be so intimidated."

After a professional-development session that featured teachers taking their peers through technology-integrated, learner-centered activities they had developed for their classes, one teacher commented that she had felt "extremely unqualified to use the technology in my classroom until today. I learned that I was doing everything that others were doing, and I learned a lot from my colleagues. Teachers shared so much. We worked on things that I could go straight into the classroom and use."

Teachers also decided to purchase software that would support their newfound uses for technology. With their representatives on the technology planning committee, these teachers fought and won the battle to purchase open-ended software rather than the drill-and-practice software purchased in the past for the computer lab.

These and other examples of an emerging community of practice at the school were evident among teachers. Teachers invited one another into their classrooms, helped each other use and plan classroom ideas around technology, and began collaborating on cross-grade activities.

The district had plans to eventually replace the older section of the building with new classrooms, but that would not happen for at least two more years. Enrique was aware of the divisions in the school among those with technology in their classrooms and those without access. "Those teachers who participated in the professional development have created a critical mass in this building. They became the 'haves' because they began to really push technology and really accomplish things, and the kids were on fire. The other teachers that were not on that level began to say, 'What about us?'"

His plan was to employ a full-time person on the campus to provide professional development and support, on demand, for all the teachers. "We need someone with Ms. Arbusto's knowledge and skills so we can continue to have a constant support process for staff over a period of time. Not only continue with the ones who have been participating, but staff that haven't had that opportunity."

Enrique wanted to encourage teachers to continue to collaborate with one another. "I've seen a lot of teaming on this campus. There are a lot of teachers matching up with each other in their classes, teachers teaming up. We have an excellent opportunity next year for those who have experience using technology and those who have not to start that teaming and mentoring process. I'm really pleased with the results that I'm seeing."

INVOLVING PARENTS AND THE COMMUNITY

Juarez Elementary had a history of involving parents, including helping them use technology. In an effort to encourage parents' comfort with technology, an initiative was implemented to loan computers to parents. First, parents were trained to use the computer, and then they were loaned a computer for a minimum of two weeks to use in their homes. These computers were typically older models, but since the school had software for these computers, parents and their children could use them at home.

Enrique, Ms. Arbusto, and the other teachers decided that another way to involve parents in their progress with technology was to host a "Cyber Parents" night. Parents could come to the school and see projects that the children had completed using technology. A free enchilada dinner was offered to those who attended.

Enrique was pleased with the high turnout for this event, as the Cyber Parents event fit well with his goals for involving parents and community members with everything going on in the school. "Nothing we do in the school is a secret. We're providing opportunities for people to be exposed to all the various things that we're doing, freely, openly giving them the information. We schedule a monthly meeting, called Parent Advisory Council meetings, with the intent of providing in-depth information on a particular program and then soliciting feedback from the parents that attend the meeting in the evening."

GRADE-LEVEL COMMUNITIES OF PRACTICE

Enrique continued to expand the professional-development and technology resources to support teachers at Juarez the next year. He was able to hire a full-time technology specialist for the campus who worked with the teachers to integrate technology. Professional development and follow-up support also were provided.

Over this second year, it became apparent that unlike at Starr, with its vertical teams, and at Lafitte, with its content-area focus, teachers at Juarez tended to work most closely with the other teachers on their grade levels. Just as the second-grade teachers had bonded and built a community of practice in the first year of the project, other grade levels began to plan together. Some of the impetus for this common planning came from the dual-language program.

Using more learner-centered approaches, however, seemed to result from the professional development and the use of technology. As one teacher explained, "We were guided to use the computers more, and to me that was a motivation to go another route, to teach with another method." One teacher noted that her fears had been allayed because of Enrique's approach of inviting rather than forcing teachers to adopt and implement technology in the classroom: "At first I thought I would find a lot of stumbling blocks and then I would get turned off. But it has been so much fun because we haven't really been too stressed. But, we have been guided. And I have been very comfortable with deciding if I am ready for the next thing or if I should stop for now. I've been very comfortable."

Working together also helped relieve some of the stress. As one teacher commented, "The other teachers are doing the same thing. We share a lot and we have Ms. Kennedy, who knows so much about computers, and she is so willing to help. And we all help Ms. Duarte, who has the most trouble. We share ideas. We are very comfortable working together." This cooperation around technology integration also extended into planning centers that the teachers could share across all the classrooms.

Teachers began planning and sharing centers that would employ technology in thematic units because some of them were having difficulty finding ways to have some of the students go to the computers while the teacher worked with the other students. "It was too difficult for them and too difficult for me going back and forth. We realized we have to make it work for them to go to the computers every day. And centers worked."

The grade-level teams decided what the thematic units would be for the year, who would develop each unit, and when they would teach it. Units developed by individual teachers included one on César Chávez, one on weather, one on Día de los Muertos (Day of the Dead) involving mathematics and social studies, and one on Mexican cowboys. The weather center required students to record weather information collected from the Internet each day. The center on Mexican cowboys was timed to coincide with a rodeo held in the community. "We share our centers. And next year we will have them ready. Many ideas are going back and forth [as we are] trying to find the ones that work. It has been a lot of work, and we are including technology."

Some of the grade levels also implemented what they called "block parties." On these days, the entire grade level would get together for some common activities across all different types of classes—the monolingual classes, the dual-language classes, and the bilingual classes. Teachers shared responsibility for planning the activities for these days.

The skills students had learned the previous year at the grade levels below them also pushed the teachers to learn and implement more. "Kids don't need as much help this year. They've already done it somewhere else. Inspiration [a computer program], they learned it last year. So, they taught me. I think every year our kids will be smarter when it comes to technology. We don't have to start at square one again."

SUSTAINING A COMMUNITY OF PRACTICE

The communities of practice built on the campus have supported the ongoing implementation of technology integration. Even though some teachers have left the school and others have come to the school, they continue to implement technology across the curriculum. They continue to come together and work together, team-teach, and create cross-grade and school-wide activities. And they have stayed together.

They have also sought other partners to help them realize their goals. The local university invited Ms. Arbusto (who was taking classes at the time) and Juarez Elementary to partner on a U.S. Department of Education technology grant. This project provided more professional development and a laptop computer for participating teachers at Juarez. Two teachers on the campus became certified as Intel Teach to the Future trainers and provided professional development for forty teachers in the district.

Cyber Parents nights have continued, allowing students to display their work using technology for their parents and the community. Students now run these events, organizing and advertising them, setting up the cafeteria for the displays, putting out the computers, and then working at the tables to teach parents how to use the technology the students learn in the classroom. Enrique explains the value of such events: "It is a powerful process when children are able to teach an adult family member how to operate a computer."

As Enrique predicted, the changes he envisioned for Juarez Elementary would take time to bear fruit. He has continued to work with the district and his staff, as well as others in the district, to realize his vision. Each year since the start of the technology-integration efforts, the school has continued to improve its scores on statewide assessments. By the time children who had been continuously enrolled in Juarez from the beginning of this initiative were in fourth, fifth, and sixth grades, scores on the state's standard assessments were equal to, or just slightly below, those reported for the best schools in the state, with the exception of fifth-grade mathematics.[1] However, fifth-grade reading scores exceeded those of the top schools in the state.

The principal summarized his philosophy, "I'll do anything that's legal to provide the children with what they need—to have the skills and knowledge they need. I won't break the law, but I'll do anything I can to provide that. And technology is a critical piece." Enrique's vision that— no matter what—the students at Juarez will be provided the highest-quality education available appears to have become a reality.

NOTE

1. According to data on the Just for the Kids Web site. Available at: http://www.just4kids.org.

7

Conclusion: Change and Communities of Practice

This book has discussed how professional development, particularly when it emphasizes using technology to improve instruction, can help teachers move from largely isolated, private practice toward a more communally based practice characterized by ongoing teacher communication, cooperation, and collaboration focused on improving instruction. These communities of practice, as they have been defined in this book, are the most effective tool for improving both the educational opportunities and the achievement of the students in the schools they serve and for ensuring that this improvement is embedded in teacher practice—and that it is institutionally sustained once professional development has ceased.

The emergence of the communities of practice discussed in this book was characterized by three phases of varying duration. Initially teachers came together as a community of interest—a purposeful collection and network of professionals formed around a new idea, common problem, or interest—using technology to promote instructional change. Communities of interest provided a social context in which learning about this area of interest could occur.

These communities of interest incrementally evolved into communities of learning, focusing on the acquisition, synthesis, and transmission of new information and on the participants as learners. The key features of these communities were communication and shared learning. Community members came together and talked about issues such as instruction, curriculum, and the use of technology. They met together regularly in both formal and informal settings and began to examine their own practice.

Once teachers began to systematically apply learning to their own classroom practice in an ongoing, sustained manner, these communities of learning became communities of practice. These communities of practice were task- and performance-oriented, focused on teacher behavior, action, and the application of knowledge and skills to classroom practice. In this stage, teachers collaborated to help one another improve the learning process and manage the implementation of innovations—and they supported one another through these changes. They were not just learning from and with one another and their students; they were also *doing*—changing instructional practice based on what was learned.

Any type of teacher community is desirable because it provides a social and professional context that formalizes learning. Communities of learning and practice can coexist, overlap, and contain the same set or subsets of members or individuals. However, although a community of learning is an absolute requisite for a community of practice, it does not constitute a community of practice until members take action in a collaborative and ongoing way. And for the purposes of school change, all communities are not equal. If schools want to promote and sustain change, assure teacher buy-in, and promote accountable implementation of what is learned in professional development, they must foster conditions that create campus-based teacher communities of practice.

WHY CREATE COMMUNITIES OF PRACTICE?

Communities of practice can provide multiple benefits that promote change on a classroom or school-wide level. In school-improvement initiatives, a community of practice can help reinforce the learning of skills and new belief systems intended to support school improvement. They provide the social support networks needed to translate learning into action. Working together, colleagues can help one another think critically about the curriculum, plan new teaching methods, use data to inform instruction, and build relationships with students.

Communities of practice make public a repertoire of agreed-on practice. Professional cooperation and collaboration replace the isolation faced by many teachers and lay the groundwork for professional sharing, feedback, and alignment between a school's vision and actual classroom practices. And as this book illustrates, these communities can then contribute to improved outcomes for students.

HOW CAN COMMUNITIES OF PRACTICE BE DEVELOPED?

Because communities of practice provide the supports and structure to help teachers change what they do, they are instrumental in any type of school-wide change. As the three school case studies illustrate, change is a highly personal and often idiosyncratic process that, despite similar inputs, can yield quite distinct outputs. Factors such as administrative and teacher leadership, a shared vision, and even individual personalities and circumstances helped to forge the creation of communities of practice in the schools examined in this book. Thus it is important to acknowledge that successful communities of practice (and successful change) may sometimes be the result of alchemy as well as chemistry.

Yet, the complexity of human and organizational behavior notwithstanding, a number of common factors foster change and the formation of communities of practice. These discrete but intersecting common denominators, discussed in the following sections, are by no means the only ones, but they are all essential to form a community.

Leadership

Strong leadership, by either an individual or a small group of people, was present in each of the site schools where communities of practice took root. This leadership was typically visionary, either tacitly or explicitly establishing a set of values and priorities that drove teacher behavior. These leaders were either formal (as in the case of Carolyn and her planning team at Starr Elementary, and Enrique and Ms. Arbusto at Juarez Elementary) or informal (as in the instance of Louise and a cadre of veteran teachers at Lafitte Middle School). In each instance, teachers' willingness to enter first into a community of interest and eventually into a community of practice depended greatly on these leaders' actions.

Carolyn and her planning team deliberately created a vision, articulated it clearly, and assembled the necessary elements to attain that vision. She hired teachers whose philosophy matched the vision and who were willing to devote the enormous energy and time required to come together, learn together, and act together on behalf of children. She provided professional development aligned with the vision. She celebrated teachers' accomplishments while providing solutions and support when teachers did not experience success. She created organizational patterns to support collaboration within vertical and horizontal teams and instigated the development of technology tools that would support ongoing analysis of needs and solutions.

Enrique led with his vision for a high-quality education for children, regardless of economic circumstances, with technology as a centerpiece. He enlisted the support of the district, parents, and community. And he invited, rather than forced, teachers to join him in pursuit of this vision. Like Carolyn, he provided professional development and the technological and human resources that teachers needed to implement new practices. He expected success, communicated this expectation, provided opportunities for teachers and students to showcase their successes, and celebrated their successes.

Confronted with the potential of having unfamiliar technology in her classroom, Louise decided to take a risk. She convinced her colleagues that technology was something that they had to learn (because it was mandated by the district) and needed to learn (because computers could add value to teaching and learning). Because Lafitte teachers valued her opinion regarding instructional matters, they agreed to embark on a process of change. And they learned much more than the technical skills they first thought would be the focus of their common inquiry. They learned how to learn again, they came to understand the conditions necessary for learning, and they experienced the richness that working with a team can add to the learning process. They infused this new knowledge into their working relationships with their students—and with one another.

Organizing Issue

To create communities of practice, teachers need a focal issue, problem, or idea. This organizing issue must be a "big idea"—deemed relevant to and critical for teachers' practice and offering significant complexity so that teachers are willing to come together, learn together, and act together around it. In addition, work on the issue must have discernible benefits for both teachers and students, and these benefits must be understood by all.

Within the schools profiled in this book, the organizing issue was technology and the new instructional practices demanded by its integration in the classroom. The focus of the professional development was not on helping teachers become technicians, but rather on helping them become managers of curriculum-based projects. This approach helped teachers weave technology into their practice, rather than view it as something outside the curriculum.

This type of technology-based professional development emphasized the instructional potential and representational attributes of technology while minimizing its technical features. Curriculum and instruction were the main foci of professional development, with technology in a supporting role to both. To help teachers understand how to use technology to enhance instruction and integrate it with curricular goals, professional-development providers employed a 5J framework to guide how computer technology would be addressed in professional-development sessions. The approach ensured that technology instruction within each professional-development activity would have the following characteristics:

- **Job-related:** Focused on classroom (i.e., instructional and curricular) needs

- **Just enough:** Emphasizing increased comfort, not proficiency, with computers
- **Just in time:** Providing teachers with skills as needed and focused on using only the tools they have at their immediate disposal
- **Just in case:** Encouraging teachers to plan sufficiently in the event of a computer malfunction
- **Just try it:** Applying enough pressure and support to impel teachers to use computers in their classrooms

Had professional development focused on specific skills for using particular pieces of software, once a new version or new application was created, teachers would have once again been novices. By minimizing the focus on technology skills, the 5J approach allowed teachers to focus on the "big ideas" surrounding technology—how it could support the curriculum, how it could enhance content, how it must be managed to assure equity and access for all students, and what kinds of activities and uses of technology would best promote student learning.

For schools involved in this professional-development program, the organizing issue around which communities developed was technology and instruction. For other schools it may be a new reading program or state assessments. Whatever the organizing issue, it must be deemed significant enough by both school leaders and teachers to allow teachers the time and teacher-centered professional development needed to focus on its connection to and implementation in the classroom.

A Willingness to Participate

Establishing a vision, purpose, or organizing issue around which people can focus their interest, learning, energy, and action is a key role for a leader who wishes to build a community of practice. People must, however, be willing to participate in the implementation of the vision, innovation, or organizing idea and must be willing to be active parties in the collection of individuals that organize around it.

Schools can encourage teacher participation in community building by creating a preexisting culture of ongoing learning, in which teacher learning is encouraged, valued, and rewarded and experimentation and risk taking are celebrated—even if it means making mistakes—and in which teachers are given the logistical and moral support to learn from mistakes. School leaders can offer this support through their words (in conversations with teachers) and through their deeds:

- By showing their own willingness to learn
- By rewarding risk and innovation

- By helping teachers learn from mistakes in a non-threatening and supportive manner
- By providing opportunities for teachers that encourage learning
- By offering adequate amounts of both pressure and support to encourage participation

Strong instructional leaders can be encouraged to serve as mentors and exemplars for their colleagues, both within formal professional-development activities and during the course of the school day. And a combination of intrinsic and extrinsic motivators that are both tangible (e.g., stipends) and intangible (e.g., praise) can also motivate teachers to participate in a community. However, although such motivators can serve as perks or a little something extra, they cannot and should not be teachers' only rationale for participation.

To build school-based communities of practice, school leaders must create and foster a collaborative practice by the express creation of formal mechanisms that promote collaboration (as in the creation of vertical and horizontal teacher teams at Starr) or by providing opportunities (shared planning periods) that allow for informal collaborative practices. The current middle and high school system, in which learning and teachers are departmentalized and compartmentalized, creates institutional barriers to collaboration. School leaders can mitigate or eliminate these barriers by organizing teachers into grade-level and inter–grade-level teams, providing structured common planning time with specific resulting classroom-based deliverables and activities, and by participating not as an authority but as a colleague in these meetings.

Teacher Learning/Professional Development

Professional development is an essential component of communities of practice, because it offers teachers formal opportunities for learning (within professional-development sessions), as well as informal opportunities for learning (follow-up conversations that result from professional development). The best professional development, like the best teaching, focuses not just on the acquisition of new knowledge and skills, but addresses teachers' beliefs, values, and behavior, providing the time and structure to plan, practice, reflect on, and revise what has been learned. However, to truly create a community—to bring teachers together, help them work together, and keep them together—the professional development cannot be the typical fare most commonly offered to teachers.

Teachers have come to believe that professional development is something to endure rather than to value. Professional development is often based in a deficit model that presumes teachers lack something—as determined by the school or district administrators rather than by teachers themselves. Professional-development choices are made without the voice of the teacher, without firsthand knowledge of the realities of teachers' classrooms, and often focus on single workshops that propose to teach a skill or develop knowledge. The teacher is then left to apply this new skill or knowledge in the classroom with little or no follow-up support and oftentimes no oversight or accountability. Thus teachers often report that although they attended professional development, they did not learn anything new or meaningful.

Professional development that helps teachers change practice and form communities that support these changes must be teacher-centered—cognizant of the needs of the teacher as a learner, as a practitioner, and as a person. It must be long-term, sustained, sequenced, and cumulative, and supported by constant follow-up. Teachers must be consulted about their needs, concerns, and strengths, along with their goals for their own practice, and these concerns and goals must be woven into the professional-development offering—tailor-made versus "off the rack."

Teacher-centered professional development focuses on teachers' practice in both concrete and theoretical ways. Placing teachers in the position of learners helps them to have experiences similar to those of their students. This approach provides a basis for reflection on how the teachers themselves learn and, subsequently, how this insight applies to their students. By focusing on the teachers as adult learners, teacher-centered professional development draws on the experiences of teachers before, during, and after professional-development sessions, when teachers are expected to actively experiment with their own practice.

Teacher-centered professional development follows a constant pattern of action, reflection, and application. It is active and hands-on, and focused on the critical elements of teaching and learning—communication, curriculum, content, assessment, instruction, and classroom management—providing teachers with an opportunity to observe, participate in, reflect on, plan, and practice a new innovation. Critical-reflection sessions, in particular, provide an opportunity for teachers to share new individual understandings of learning, ideas, and concerns; examine what did and did not work in the classroom and why; and speculate, reason, and critically evaluate themselves and their peers so they can make decisions based on evidence, observation, and reflection versus tradition, inertia, authority, or impulse. Opportunities for shared critical reflection help to create a common body of knowledge and philosophy on which communities of practice can be built.

With its focus on teachers' needs, teacher-centered professional development provides opportunities for building relationships by focusing on the teacher as a person, not just a professional. Relationships with the professional-development provider and with other teachers are formed through regularly scheduled interactions over a sustained period of time (in the authors' case, two years). Such relationships promote trust and a feeling of safety in trying new things as teachers begin to see their colleagues as part of a supportive community and as teacher confidence increases as a result of the successful implementation of new instructional practices.

The sense of isolation teachers often feel when they work alone in their classrooms is challenged through teacher-centered professional development. Practice becomes public as discussions with other teachers reveal the challenges faced by everyone, particularly teachers working in low-performing schools. By working in small, cooperative groups and assuming roles within them, teachers can participate in the types of learning activities promoted by the professional development while also getting to know their colleagues on a deeper level. This dynamic allows for a greater exchange of professional experiences and expectations; cultivates personal and professional connections; and makes teachers feel like part of a team focused on a common goal. These sorts of connections form the foundation of a community of practice.

Support Structures and Resources

Coming together is a beginning, but to stay together and work together, communities of practice need constant support and maintenance. Once a community of interest is formed, support structures and resources are necessary to move it forward to a community of learning and eventually a community of practice. Schools often appear to operate with the expectations that change will somehow happen, without providing the time and resources needed, and that mandating that teachers do something differently is enough. But building communities of practice is neither a quick nor inexpensive process. It takes tenacity and commitment on the part of leaders and teachers.

It also takes leaders who recognize that communities of practice do not form quickly but, rather, slowly unfold and coalesce over time as a result of frequent contact, common endeavors, and shared practice. Any type of community formation at a school level demands that teachers are provided resources, supports, incentives, time, and human networks required to learn together, practice what they have learned, and then put into practice this learning.

Members of communities of practice also need additional supports to assist them in the process of changing practice. Finding time may require supports such as reduced teaching schedules, shared planning periods with colleagues, resources (adequate hardware, software, and supplies), and the moral support of administrators, other teachers, parents, and district administrators. Schools must invest precious resources to provide the time and tools needed to make such transformations.

UNDERSTANDING CHANGE

As noted at the outset of chapter 1, this book is essentially about change—the personal, interpersonal, and institutional changes that occurred over the course of a two-year school-improvement project and the way in which teacher-centered professional development and technology played a role in that transformation.

Computers and professional development are all about change. The very nature of computer technology implies rapid change within a very short time period. Indeed, the words *computer* and *technology* are often coupled with *revolution*, although the quick pace of revolutionary change is not often associated with schools. Those who promote technological change (for example, professional-development providers) are often aware of the rapid pace of technology innovations but often bemoan the rate of *teacher* change. Yet schools are human institutions, and humans and organizations more often than not favor slow, incremental change or "progress." Schools are also tradition-bound places governed by an environment that prizes stasis and stability. Negative feedback loops (Toffler, 1970) dampen or suppress change when it threatens to exceed certain levels, helping to preserve an institutional equilibrium. In contrast, technology and professional development are driven by *positive* feedback loops, which serve not to suppress change but to accelerate and amplify it. These competing tendencies, combined with what is often an inability to challenge our prevailing cognitive models, as well as the pressures of politicians and the general public, who often feel they know better about schools than do the people running them, can make meaningful, sustained school-based change almost impossible.

Any project whose goals are the adoption and integration of technology has the potential for conflict or "future shock" (Toffler, 1970)—the stress and disorientation that arise from subjecting human beings to too much change in a short amount of time. Schools must balance the rate of human change with that demanded by the innovation (in this case, technology) and understand that although computer technology can, if properly used, transform teaching and learning, it cannot transform human nature. Human change can and will continue to be a limited and slow process, and resistance is often a psychological response to the overwhelming change and complexity associated with technology. Technology may promote revolution, but educators must aim for evolution—change that is contextually appropriate, realistic, sustained, and grounded in what works.

This is where communities of practice assume a critical role. They can help teachers fashion adaptive responses to change, create strategies to implement change incrementally and deliberatively in their classrooms, and provide some equilibrium in what can be a disorienting process. They can provide a human support network that helps members work together to adopt new practices and innovations at their own rate, degree, and frequency. They are a harbor for individuals who may resist and fear change but who also welcome it and work toward implementing it to benefit both teaching and learning.

References

Anderson, J. R. (1995). *Learning and memory.* New York: Wiley.

Barth, R. (2001). *Learning by heart.* San Francisco: Jossey-Bass.

Brandt, R. (September 1992). Building a community for learning. *Educational Leadership, 50*(1), 19–23.

Burns, M. (December 2002). From compliance to commitment: Technology as a catalyst for communities of learning. *Phi Delta Kappan, 84*(4), 295–302.

Claxton, C., & Murrell, P. (1987). *Learning styles: Implications for improving educational practices.* Washington, DC: Association for the Study of Higher Education.

Dewey, J. (1933). *How we think: A restatement of the relations of reflective thinking to the educative process.* Boston: D. C. Heath.

Dimock, K. V., Burns, M., Heath, M., & Burniske, J. (2001). *Applying technology to restructuring and learning: How teachers use computers in technology assisted constructivist learning environments.* Austin, TX: Southwest Educational Development Laboratory.

Fullan, M. (2001). *Leading in a culture of change.* San Francisco: Jossey-Bass.

Fullan, M., with Stiegelbauer, S. M. (1991). *The new meaning of educational change.* New York: Teachers College Press.

Hord, S. M. (1997). *Outcomes of professional learning communities for staff and students.* Austin, TX: Southwest Educational Development Laboratory.

Knowles, M. S. (Ed.). (1984). *Andragogy in action.* San Francisco: Jossey-Bass.

Lyons, N. (1990). Dilemmas of knowing: Ethical and epistemological dimensions of teachers' work and development. *Harvard Education Review, 60*(2), 159–180.

Martinez, M., Perez, B., & Cook, G. (1998). Key dimensions of school life. *Primary Voices K–6, 6*(1), 3–8.

National Center for Educational Accountability. *Just for the kids.* Retrieved May 2005 from http://nc4ea.org/jftk/index.cfm.

Postman, N., & Weingartner, C. (1969). *Teaching as a subversive activity.* New York: Dell.

Riel, M., & Polin, L. (2004). Learning communities: Common ground and critical differences in designing technical support. In S. A. Barab, R. Kling, & J. Gray (Eds.), *Designing for virtual communities in the service of learning.* Cambridge, MA: Cambridge University Press.

Rogers, E. (1995). *Diffusions of innovation.* New York: Free Press.

Senge, P. (1990). *The fifth discipline.* London: Doubleday.

Toffler, A. (1970). *Future shock.* New York: Random House.

Wenger, E. (1998). Communities of practice: Learning as a social system. *Systems Thinker.* Retrieved May 2005 from http://www.co-i-l.com/coil/knowledgegar den/cop/lss.shtml.

Index

81; communities of practice and, 21, 30–33; curriculum and, 22, 40, 46, 62, 75, 80; database, 55, 60–63, 65; experts, 22, 25–28, 31–32, 37, 43–44; fear of, 1, 12, 16, 22, 25–27; learning and, 24–25, 37, 52, 58, 67, 71–72, 74; teams, 26, 33, 37, 39–41, 73, 75, 79; testing and, 35, 41–42, 44, 49–50, 59–63

thematic units, 53–57, 65, 74–75

Toffler, A. (Alvin), 85

U.S. Department of Education technology grant, 75

veteran teachers. *See* teachers, veteran
vision, vii, 6, 13, 26, 49–65, 67–70, 76, 78–79, 81

Wenger, E., 5

About the Authors

Mary Burns is a senior technology specialist at Education Development Center, where she designs professional development programs, creates teacher curriculum and delivers professional development to help teachers, teacher trainers and school administrators use technology to improve instruction. Mary's work has taken her to the Caribbean, Latin America, and the Middle East and she presently works primarily in Asia and Africa. Mary spent six years at SEDL helping to design and deliver the professional development described in this book and taught ten years in middle and high schools in the US and in Jamaica.

K. Victoria Dimock is a program director at the Southwest Educational Development Laboratory (SEDL) in Austin, Texas where she directs work aimed at improving school performance and improving teaching and learning in mathematics, science, and technology. She has conducted research and provided professional development for educators for the past twenty years.